The American Wild Turkey and Why I Don't Have One By Jacob Pistner Is a short and sweet journey through turkey hunting and conservation.

Roland Welker
100 Day King/Alone SE-7
History Channel

I have been hunting for over sixty years and didn't know there was so much I didn't know about turkeys. I have shot a lot of turkeys in my time, but for someone like Jacob not to have harvested a turkey, his writing has much wit, with his little funny puns and his background of research.

There were times while reading I could relate to his stories, like the fox that snuck up on him. The same thing happened to me when I was leaning up against a log and heard a russell (which woke me up I have shot a lot of turkeys sitting still while taking a nap, and it was a fox coming up the log).

By reading Jacob's book, I see he has put his time in the woods, and I'm glad to see where his heart is not just in bagging a turkey, but the whole experience that he writes about.

Jeff & Janet Colwell
Hicks Run Outfitters

The North American Wild Turkey
and
Why I Don't Have One

Jacob Pistner

The North American Wild Turkey and Why I Don't Have One

© 2026 Jacob Pistner

All rights reserved. No part of this publication may be reproduced, distributed, or transmitted in any form by any means, including photocopying, recording, or other electronic methods without the prior written permission of the author, except in the case of brief quotations embodied in reviews and certain other noncommercial uses permitted by copyright law. For permission requests, bulk orders, or speaking requests, please write to the author at the address below.

Printed in the United States of America

First Printing, March 2026

Paperback ISBN:979-8-9991650-6-0

Ebook ISBN: 979-8-9943733-0-9

Cover Design and Layout: Katie Zeliger

Interior Formatting: Kathryn Jordan

Meraki Press LLC
www.merakipress.org

Jacob Pistner is an avid outdoorsman from Elk County, Pennsylvania.

nawt_book@yahoo.com

For My Lovely Wife, Hope.

Contents

Forward	1
Part 1: Backward	8
1.1 The Father	16
1.2 An Early Pursuit	24
1.3 Disease	32
Part 2: The Birds Around Us	48
2.1 Potential Danger	56
2.2 Across the Rio Grande	67
2.3 The Gould Standard	73
2.4 Midstate Majesty	80
2.5 A Panhandle Hottie	86
2.6 Sworn Enemies	92
Part 3: Hunting the Elusive Turkey	100
3.1 Calling for the Big One	104
3.2 Hiding is an Art Form	111
3.3 Gauge Your Confidence	116

3.4 People Are Strange	125
Part 4: In Conclusion and for Conservation	135
4.1 I'm Not Done Yet	143
About the Author	149

Forward

As I begin the writing process of this book, it is to be noted that at this time of my life I remain *turkeyless.* Not every hunter is successful when it comes to the harvest, and I personally don't think killing is priority number one when I am in the woods. But turkey hunting for me is growing tiresome.

Some hunters go out in the woods to avoid their families (I mean, for time alone in the wilderness; it is a good way to de-stress and have time to self-reflect). Other hunters march out into the fields and mountains because they love the outdoors and the animals they pursue. Many of those hunters are students of nature and have strong ideologies about the wheres and whens of harvesting an animal. Tactics, locations, and gear are always up for hot debate (or often even argument) amongst them. Many members of the hunting community who go out into the woods with the intent of harvesting an animal are attempting to strengthen or build their connection with God. The created world around us is a beautiful thing and can be quite powerful for the spirit. Then there is the reality that many, many others are just filling the freezer to get by for another season. It is an honest truth that a lot of the people around us are just trying to feed their families in one way or another. Heck, we should all be able to agree that most, if not all, the animals we harvest on our own probably lived a better life than some slaughterhouse pig or chicken we mindlessly eat on any given occasion. So, let's not jump to bashing food security for these select people.

For each of these possible situations a hunter may be in, I would call the act of hunting noble in its own way. The value of hunting isn't always gauged by the kill but rather by what someone gains from the experience. A "trophy animal" will be described very differently by each hunter. Even some of the great thinkers and authors in history recognized and reflected on these concepts. Henry David Thoreau is quoted as saying, "*Many men go fishing all of their lives without knowing that it is not fish they are after.*"[1] (I know it's not a hunting quote, but try to stick with me here.)

Believe it or not, hunting is more than what some imagine to be just a teenager's bloodlust. It's good to remind ourselves and people of the general population, including the anti-hunter, of this notion. Many hunters started young in their hunting careers so they could be taught by an elder friend or family member important lessons of life, stewardship, and respect for nature, for example. I would be willing to bet that most young hunters go through a phase where the kill is some monumental moment of their life; it's absolutely an adrenaline rush to kill your first target, and there is no way to say it any differently. If a hunter doesn't get excited, why even bother? Once these hunters gain more experience, there is still plenty of excitement to go around, but the kill quickly becomes just part of the process. Soon, we learn to reflect on the hunt itself and the effort that went into the challenge of harvesting the animal that now lies before us. I remember when I shot my first squirrel with my dad. I was so excited, and the adrenaline was so intense that my legs turned to jello. I had to sit down for a while. My dad had a good laugh about it, to my embarrassment, of course. When I think about that day, the squirrel has now—years later—become wildly important to me because I got to enjoy time with family out in the woods, and then later at the dinner table.

It doesn't take anyone very long to recognize that hunting has a lot of purpose and meaning to it. Hunting is important to many of the families that partake in it, and traditions quickly get built around the process. On a larger scale, whether someone likes it or not, culturally, hunting has been part of our very long human history. We have to eat, and hunting practices affect everything from farming to animal herds, logging practices, and legislation—just to name a few things. It's no wonder that in Pennsylvania, we say "Watch for deer!" instead of "Goodbye!" when you leave a party. It's part of the culture. Dedicated and forward-thinking hunters can do a lot for our communities when it comes right down to it. So be sure to thank a hunter next time you *don't* crush a deer or turkey on your next ride home.

So, now that you're one (lengthy) set of paragraphs into this, it's okay to think, "this author can't put a bird to bed because he is some philosophical '*jag-off.*'" Let me take a moment to remind everyone that we can't all be *Tenth Legion* author and turkey aficionado Tom Kelly, knocking down birds at the resilient old age of ninety-something when we just damned well feel like it. I have spent my time out in the woods, and fields, and mountains, and hills, and valleys, and stream beds... must I go on? So, let me be clear: all this self-reflection isn't from a lack of trying. The turkey just seems to elude me.

As a northern Pennsylvania mountain hunter, I am used to the disappointment the Alleghenies give us from season to season. However, the scenery is never disappointing. High mountains and plateaus adorned in sporadic deep green hemlock forests, streams and rivers quietly flowing from every nook and cranny you can find, and old infrastructure such as logging roads, coal strippings, and so much more will keep the imagination busy for the entirety of the hunt. Pennsylvania is truly breathtaking. Finding the target animal, though—now that is a different story. There have always been times when I'm worried the deer I passed up will be the last one I will see that year, and it's happened. It's tough in these mountains, and I'm sure if I found almost any other outdoorsmen around this part of my beloved PA, they would agree. Many hunters have fallen on hard times due to over-hunting and destruction, or lack of habitat for this animal or that one. (Does that sound familiar, *Potter County*?)

If I wanted to tell someone how great I was at something, I'd write a book on trout or bass fishing, but I suppose once I gave away all my secrets, that would be ruined for me in no time! So, here I am, scribbling away for some reason, obsessed with what is arguably my biggest shortcoming as a hunter.

Then why write about turkey hunting?

The truth is, I am infatuated with this avian survival machine, and the sheer fact that, for some reason, I haven't been able to harvest one. What is it about their ability to survive and overcome the dangers of the forest? Whether it be predators, hard terrain, or people, all over North America, these birds are successful in conquering the hardships they endure. All while getting along as a cumbersome, surprisingly vocal, and semi-flightless bird. Survival for them sure doesn't look easy at first glance.

Most of the time, regardless of the bird being male or female, I hear them and can locate them before I ever see them (or never see them) at all. Sometimes it's the loud gobbles or just the little "purrs" and "putts" that they make as they feed that give them away. Other occasions, it's the crazy loud flapping of their ungainly wings as they come barreling down from the evening's roost.

How are they ultimately able to survive in almost any portion of North America, and why the hell can't I get one in range of my shotgun? The turkey seems to know all in its domain, and I am just its victim of circumstance. Maybe this very thought of survival crossed Ben Franklin's mind when he once wrote to his daughter saying, "...*a much more respectable Bird [than the eagle] and withal a true Native of America... he is besides though, a little vain and silly, a Bird of Courage.*" [2] He hit the nail on the head in so few words. There is a lot of historical rumor around Ben Franklin's love for the wild turkey. It is even said that he rallied Congress in an attempt to make it the national bird, as he felt it represented the American people more closely than the eagle. Some say that this and the whole letter to his daughter are just satire or even fake, but for all intents and purposes, I'm going with it.

So, even our forefathers knew that the turkey was something special here, even if they did not pursue it as a game animal. I can't recall anyone ever saying

Ben Franklin was an avid hunter (unless, of course, we count chasing the ladies). They recognized the gall of this oddly beautiful animal and what it would mean to the many people inhabiting the new world. I think that these people must have soon felt the same, as it's no surprise that the turkey is still here to this day. As I write the contents of this book, I'll continue my journey to not only take a bird for myself, but to better understand the reality that this animal lives in. I would also like to state that by drawing attention to the five species of North American Wild Turkey, I will hopefully inspire others to enjoy the hunt and what it has to offer them. We need to conserve the birds' habitat and the beautiful places they live so future generations can get out and enjoy the hunt as well. I'll encourage this, regardless of how lucky (or, in my current case, *unlucky*) I may be as a hunter.

Part 1: Backward

With a lack of successful turkey hunts in my life, there comes an abundance of time in between seasons to think about them. I'd have to argue that if I am going to sit here and try to convince someone of where I plan to go with all of this, I will have to at least fill them in on where I have been. By no means is this book supposed to be some sort of "woe is me, the ailing turkey hunter!" autobiographical text, but people probably need some information on why *I think* this is now a worthy way to spend their time. Lord knows any of us could just be out hunting turkey right now, instead of reading about me being terrible at it.

Turkey hunting has made me a better hunter in general, and it has put me much more in tune with the woods and what is going on around me while I'm there. There are little nuances that can be learned from this pursuit, like listening to the differences in sounds heard in the depths of the forest. For example, a female hen is approaching. Is she feeding? Looking for a mate? Or warning the flock of some immediate danger? There is a big difference in those *putts* and *clucks* that the novice hunter hears versus the deep language turkeys have, heard by the experienced woodsman. Hunters quickly start to hear the difference between turkeys' personalities, and it really reinforces the idea that each of these creatures is their own singular being. I wouldn't say "just like us," but it's definitely in their own way.

That's probably the number one reason why they're so hard to hunt; each of them is unique. It's challenging to target some mountain bird on this or that hillside, or another in a clear cut, as they might respond differently to a hunter's approach. Turkeys may also respond to other natural triggers going on around them and change their direction, feeding habits, or response to calling attempts, regardless of what we are trying to get them to do.

How again does this correlate to other areas of hunting and make me and other turkey hunters better woodsmen in general?

Well, let's think again about the other sounds we hear out in the woods. Here is another example: the sound of footprints. Twelve-year-old me would jump out of his boots when he heard a squirrel approaching or digging through the leaves. The *swish swish* sound made by the squirrel in the leaves is far distinguished from the rhythmic hooves of an approaching whitetail. These two sounds are much different than a turkey digging through the leaves to find some good bugs (something I wouldn't have ever comprehended as an adolescent). Something as simple as the rustling of leaves is something that has to be learned to be separated from *actual* animal sounds. Heck, I have even mistaken what was really a bear walking through the brush out of the sheer hope that it was actually the buck of a lifetime knocking his clunky, ungodly antlers off of every tree branch he had the misfortune of coming across. That's probably a story for another book, which I would title something like, "Bear Hunting: Don't Stand So Close to Me." I'll indulge in a bear story later in this book, but we won't get too carried away just yet.

Turkey hunting encourages a person to be still. We take in so much around us when we are trying to hide from the world. This is a skill that all people of this earth should take some time to master, hunter or non-hunter. Being still clears the mind and lets us focus on what is going on with ourselves and our bodies. Think of yoga, but there is a shotgun nearby, and no one has to stick their butt up in the air. Kind of a win-win for all of us!

Seriously, being still allows us to take in a lot of information. I actually get a chance to notice exactly when and where the sun comes up and which hillside gets light first. I actually listen to the songs of the songbirds, caws of the crow, and hear the owls ask, "who, who cooks for you?" I have quickly learned to pinpoint movement in the brush and anticipate where an animal may be coming from. I see the squirrels and chipmunks working their food caches and take time to observe where their homes are and what nuts and berries they are feeding on. Taking in this kind of information helps me, and many others, plan the hunt for whatever the next animal may be, turkey or not. If the weather is cold, I look for that first sunny hillside. A critter is sure to peek out there and warm up. If the squirrels are moving, I like to approach areas where they feed with caution so they don't sound the alarm. Squirrels are rowdy, and if they don't like someone, they will tell everyone nearby, friend or foe. Most importantly, the lesson that I have learned from all of this is not to just "be still" but to "be still and listen."

The unique experiences of being still are something that will last a lifetime. I have had multiple occasions where a big mother doe brings her newborn, softly-spotted fawn right next to me and starts feeding while I am hunkered up against a tree stump. She will never know I am there, hiding against the rough bark of an old tree, and it gives me time to study them. I enjoy watching the new life she made buck, jump, and play in an open cornfield while she watches closely over them with her protective eye. It's really a beautiful thing to see.

My favorite of all still moments, though, was during a spring turkey hunt while I was sitting along a cut cornfield near a friend's home. I had recently eaten a pack of fruit snacks, my preferred hunting treat, and I was taking in some sunshine while resting against a big tree that served as a part of a windbreak between fields. Turkey hunting that morning was slow, and against my better judgment, I decided to go for a longer walk and try a new spot. I was exhausted, and my backpack was lying on the ground beside me, wide open because of my sometimes lazy demeanor while I am out turkey hunting. Even though hunting is good exercise, I also use opportunities like this to relax my mind and body.

While soaking in the rays, I could see tall grass rustling to my right-hand side. I carefully watched as I was approached by a dark and slender mink. As members of the weasel family, these curious and sometimes aggressive little critters are highly sought after by fur trappers all over North America. They are also pretty rare where I hunt, as Pennsylvania only has a population of approximately 30,000 members. To my surprise, whether the mink noticed me or not, he came within inches of my legs and curiously looked around for a moment, studying me. Without any further notice, he jumped right into my open backpack! After a couple seconds of rustling around, he sprang out as if to say, "Hey! There isn't anything in here left to eat!" He gave me a hard look and, without any hesitation, was onto the next adventure as quickly as he started the last.

Watching this take place and having the privilege of replaying this in my head over and over through the years is one of the coolest experiences I think a person could have. Forget the rollercoasters and lines. Forget flying for hours to sit in a hotel somewhere. Forget sitting in the same old cookie-cutter restaurant pretending their house wine is decent, and go actually observe what's in the world around us! This mink was a one of a kind. No one has that memory or experience but me, and I will always hold that in a special place as I think back about my years in the woods. Being still and taking the time to observe nature is what gave me that experience. A memory like this is something a person can only create by going out in the wilderness and buying into what the world is offering them.

Lastly, as we get into the background of all this, I need to touch on the inspiration behind writing this book. I know it sounds like I have been hunting turkey for fifteen years by the way I'm willing to whine and complain about my journey to knock down some big tom. But honestly, at the time I started this book, it was only my fourth turkey season. During these four turkey hunting seasons, I had a big change in my thought process when it came to the approach to hunting. This was due to several life events that included a non-hunting-related injury I sustained during my time as a competitive runner and coach.

Outside of lifestyle changes that came from that, I was also heavily influenced by another author and entrepreneur named Steven Rinella. He has his hands in a few things. Steve is a best-selling author, podcaster, and TV show personality known for his series "MeatEater," and I think he does a great job of bringing an educated approach to the sport of hunting. His show and stories are far more about the adventure and pursuit of the animal than the actual kill. There is no goofball mumbo-jumbo in his show that the classic hunting shows I would have seen on TV as a kid had. I have never believed that there is validation behind sitting along a game preserve's fence, and then praising God for some animal that was lined up for its doom to collect good television ratings. I want to barf just thinking about it, and I am sure the anti-hunters do too.

Many of Rinella's stories end in sharing a good meal, telling stories of the hunt, promoting conservation of the animal or land, or sometimes just self-reflection and lessons learned. I respect any man or woman who can take their experiences and build upon them in some form or another, or take time to share them with friends and family. Watching Steve hunt turkeys and discuss the characteristics of their nature with his friends and other acquaintances romanticized the experience of hunting them and encouraged me to try something new. I quickly gravitated to his content on the ins and outs of turkey hunting, and it immediately had me hooked on the idea that I need to get out there and try it.

Thanks to his bit of insight, focus on conservation, and positive voice for the sport that Rinella lends to us through his content, I decided to give this whole turkey hunting thing a try. Plus, I had a couple of good friends who thought they would take this on with me.

All we had to do was hunt birds, right?

Easy!

Little did I know what was ahead of me in this endeavor.

1.1 The Father

My dad *hated* hunting turkey.

That's it. As a twelve-year-old boy, all I knew was that *we* didn't want to wake up at 3:00 a.m. to "hunt some old stinky bird." So in turn, we didn't. He has always been quite the outdoorsman, ever busy with this thing or that thing or the other thing, and has a deep passion for getting out in the woods. As a kid, my dad and I would regularly hunt for pheasant, grouse, squirrels, and—religiously—whitetail. But why we never went out for turkey is beyond me.

I used to read numerous articles in his lifetime membership magazine, *North American Hunting Club*, a now-defunct organization (1978–2013). The texts were always something focused on the conservation of land, personal hunting stories, and hunting anecdotes. Conveniently located on the bay window sill of our living room, I'd regularly sit and thumb through articles, hang out with the family dog, and play Game Boy. (Now you can really picture the true child of the early 2000's that I am.)

The great Jim Shockey himself wrote my favorite articles, and he always found a way to tie humor and fun into his experiences as an outdoorsman (always on the last page as a bookend, if I remember correctly). I'd like to think that many of the stories I tell about hunting with my dad and brother share similarities with some of the silly tongue-in-cheek takes on life that Shockey wrote about. His articles were my first real interest in hunting content, and they felt relatable.

There was always something going on around the house or in our lives that would pull us into the outdoor world while we were growing up, whether it was reading, hunting, fishing, or otherwise. My grandmother on my dad's side was also an enthusiast of the animals that lived around her home, and she shared that with him and us as children. In turn, it built a generational interest in the wildlife that surrounded our family. It was also convenient that my grandparents lived in the old family camp, and we had what felt like an endless amount of land to explore in our youth. For most of my life, my dad (or "The Bear Master," as some have known him) would rather go fishing in some of the great trout waters we have in Northern PA than wait for some dirty old turkey to gobble. As I mentioned before, fishing is a shared favorite pastime of mine as well, but I can't be wasting time writing about that right now.

He did an exceptional job of getting me interested in the world of hunting. Over the years, as I got more and more eager to be in the woods and challenge myself, I've expanded into other areas of the sport. He, of course, has settled down some since then, but we still share a lot of the same interests. Regardless, turkey hunting still eludes him to this day, and as polar opposite as we sometimes are, it remains my primary obsession.

When I was on probably my first (if not second) rifle hunt for whitetail deer during Pennsylvania's youth doe season, I remember plenty of the tests he would put me through. All day long, we would climb hill after hill, through the woods, fallen leaves littered the ground, making it tricky to see what I was stepping on. How do I not step on the sticks and break them? And how do I maneuver about the slippery moss growing at the edges of the stones and stumps?

"Which way home is camp?" He would ask me. I spent some time thinking about it, and I'd confidently point in the direction I felt was best. "No, it's that way." He would point in the complete opposite direction. "Heel-toe, heel-toe..." he would tell me when my footsteps got too loud. My boots were heavy as hell back then. I can still hear him saying it in my sleep. These and many other tests occurred as he built his trust in me as a young hunter and, ultimately, a man. These are important lessons learned and taught me that "this hunting thing isn't always easy."

I thought deer were just going to be bursting at the seams out there. Every time we got into a brushy area, I was convinced that there would be a shooter buck (one side of the antlers has to have three points or more) or a nice doe, and I would get the big payoff that I was working toward in no time. Time after time, sit after sit, drive after drive, I would see a tail here, a glimpse there, but there was never any shooting. It was a tough start.

For several years, Pennsylvania split up its doe and buck seasons and had a dedicated youth doe hunting season on top of that. I was of legal age for the youth season, and on one of my first trips out, we found ourselves in a unique situation. It was late in the day during this specific hunt, and my dad and I were casually meandering our way down an old logging trail. We were lightly chatting, and he stopped me midway through my sentence. Standing at a low point on the hill, we were surrounded by hardwood trees in a manner that almost looked like they were placed there on purpose. Blackberry bushes and beech brush obscured my vision, but I was just tall enough to see over what we call "thrashings." When I got my wits about me, he directed me to look up on the side hill, and I could see that there were two beautiful bucks, bedded down together getting their last few minutes of sunbathing in. A six-point on the left and an eight-point on the right, both illegal to harvest, and they couldn't have cared less if we were there. I always get this feeling that animals can sense if they are in danger or not and when something's off. In this case, the deer were as safe as could be, and so they stayed there, enjoying their time together in the late-day sunshine. My evening ended with one last quiet hike up the hill to camp. It's a shame neither is hanging on my wall, but we set some silly rules as humans. That day, doe season was doe season, and that's that! If rules like this weren't in place, there probably wouldn't be any deer left to hunt. I don't know if you ever noticed, but historically, humans haven't practiced moderation well.

As one can imagine, these two sunbathing bucks only added to my disappointment, but I learned an important lesson: the hunt is never over! As long as I'm in the woods, anything can happen, and that is one of the major factors that contributes to my continued hunt for my first turkey. If I keep getting out there, anything can happen. Be it any sport, craft, or hobby, as long as someone is immersed in it, good things will eventually come to them as long as they remain engaged.

To finish out the story, later that season some luck came to us. During the regular rifle season, my dad and I were set up in a two-man tree stand. This was homemade, of course, and for all imaginative purposes, picture two handsomely rugged dudes dressed like the great pumpkin suspended ten feet in the air. We were even so lucky that we had seats made from old and *very* comfortable five-gallon buckets. Ah, the sweet life it was. An afternoon of sitting yielded little action for the day. There was some conversation between us (mostly him telling me to sit still), and I tried not to eat all my snacks right away.

My dad always taught me not to look for a whole deer when glassing an area. For those unfamiliar, I was scanning with a scope or binoculars to try and find my target animal and sometimes check out a bird or two. So out of boredom, I started challenging myself.

Is it a leaf or an ear?
Was that a bird or a tail flicker?
Who knows? Anything can happen.

And then it did! My heart was about to explode (and I think my body temperature rose to a dangerous level). It took all the focus and breath I had to say quietly to my dad, "I think I can see a doe's head over there," gesturing to the brush in front of us. He picked out the deer immediately, and to my surprise, I was right. "Two ribs back from the shoulder." That's the only thought that went through my head as I brought my dad's .222 Savage to my shoulder.

I set it up as best I could, holding tight and trying to control my breathing. Before I could wrap my head around it all, the safety was off, and I carefully squeezed the trigger. The crack of the gun going off rang in my ears, and I felt the hard kick of the stock against my bony twelve-year-old shoulder. From there, it felt like an out-of-body experience. As I looked through the scope, I saw the deer jump. I knew that I hit her, and my adrenaline doubled as she quickly disappeared into the brush. The first time someone harvests a big game animal under their own conditions, it's a shock to the system. I was physically shaking and felt hot like I had a fever. Sitting beside me, I think my dad was more excited than I was.

Now the task of finding her began.

After a good bit of tracking, we found the beautiful doe lying in the tall winter grasses below a power line. All I could think about was how excited I was to show my grandparents and to have my dad see me now as a man. Every steak, piece of jerky, and jar of canned meat was mine. It was because of me. It was big. I am forever grateful for that deer's gift, and I have been forever hooked on hunting. (Hooked—I know, another fishing reference, but remember we aren't here to talk about that.)

All in all, my dad did a great job getting me started in my general hunting career, but never fostered the urge to turkey hunt. To this day, he has never taken me up on a turkey hunt, mainly because "What the heck am I going to do with it?" is his excuse. Kudos to him, though. Let's not bother to shoot something we aren't going to enjoy eating.

My love for the woods and its creatures runs deep, and my time there is always best shared with friends and family. So take someone hunting, a little brother or sister, the neighbor kid, even grandpa. Doesn't matter! Get someone out there and share the world with them like my dad did for me. Even if someone isn't going after an animal as game, it can be worth a lifetime of memories. Getting a camera out, going spotting on a warm fall evening, or just watching whatever walks or flies under the bird feeder can be a wonderful experience for someone to have. That's what makes it all worth it.

1.2 An Early Pursuit

One of the longest nights of my entire life was, by far, the night before my first turkey hunt. We were teenagers, barely past driving age (you're allowed to hunt without an adult in Pennsylvania when you turn sixteen), when a close friend of mine, Sean, convinced me that turkey hunting would be worth my while. I remained, at this time, a skeptic of turkey hunting due to my family influences, despite my buddy's efforts to convert me into a turkey hunting machine.

Sean was a regular among the neighbor kids when I was growing up. He was a little cousin of one of the boys we ran around with, and almost exactly my age. Sean became an avid hunter over the years, thanks to the influence of his grandfather, and he thrived on turkey hunting. During hunting seasons, we would regularly send each other text messages and pictures while sitting in the brush somewhere, or from the birds-eye view of a treestand as we gave each other updates on the hunt. Usually, we wouldn't have much to show other than trees and leaves, but nevertheless, we have been doing this even into our thirties. Having opportunities to hunt close to home and at several family members' camps, he bagged a bird for the first time early in his teens. Once he got the bug for "the old dirty bird," Sean was determined to change my mind about hunting them. Anyone who knew him back then would say that if nothing else, he was convincing, and the offer to hunt turkeys was hard to resist.

We went out in spring gobbler season (Pennsylvania holds two seasons: a fall turkey, where hunters can harvest a hen or gobbler, and a spring gobbler, where they can only take a bearded bird) and worked out a Saturday that wouldn't conflict with family and work schedules. Teenagers are very busy for some reason, but we found time. Sean lived on the outskirts of town, bordering a few of the small farms in our area, and he had permission to hunt the one adjacent to his parents' home. Freshly cut and soon-to-be-planted farmland is always a good place to start for turkey hunting (be sure to get permission from the landowner), as the birds will often come out to feed in the early hours of the day. It also gives a big tom somewhere to strut his stuff and get a look at nearby hens and potential competitors. Sean assured me that he had an area scouted far back on the farm, and we were guaranteed a shot at a bird. After a Friday night dinner, I grabbed my shotgun and camouflage clothing and headed in his direction. In Pennsylvania, during the first half of spring gobbler season, you can only hunt birds during the morning hours until noon, so a morning hunt was our only option. On this particular Friday night, both Sean's and my efforts were limited to one last scouting of the fields, while I just got familiar with the new spot.

After dropping off my gear, avoiding any conversation with parents or siblings that might take up time, we hopped on his four-wheeler and rode out to the back end of the farm. He drove, and I sat on the hard metal rack at the rear.

"No one hunts here." He sounded confident. We were so sure that the back field was ours and ours alone. (*Yeah, I know*—there's some classic foreshadowing.) As we rode back, there were a series of blueberry bushes, strawberry fields, and cut corn stalks. It looked pretty good to me at first glance. And *oh boy,* was it.

The path crested the hill on the right-hand side when we entered the back field. One of the largest flocks of turkey I have ever seen to this day—forty plus birds—saw us coming on the four-wheeler. In a panic, they started running, flying, and changing directions as fast as they could. Many of them went right down the path in front of us, and when we approached them, they took off into the air and flew over the cut corn. As soon as we came up on the birds, they disappeared into the darkness of the hardwood forest in front of us. My mind remembers it in slow motion, even though this took only a few seconds. We got so close, I practically thought I could have reached out and grabbed a turkey by its tail feathers. There were turkeys everywhere, just waiting to be someone's dinner. *This was going to be too easy*.

We shut off the four-wheeler, scouted the edges of the field for some game trails where animals may have been moving in and out, and then finally picked out the spots we wanted to sit in for the morning. After experiencing what finding buried treasure must be like, we exchanged our excitement for the next morning of hunting and headed back to the house.

I had a rough night ahead of me. It was undisclosed to me that we were going to wake up at 3:00 a.m. to prepare for the long morning ahead of us. I am usually a person who experiences some nerves before a big event to begin with, and thinking about our evening—and now planning for an early wake-up—didn't help much. Probably too many handfuls of salt and vinegar chips and cans of pop didn't help me sleep that night either. Even when I ran competitively, it didn't matter if it was a 5K or half marathon; I probably ruined more races due to lack of sleep than I would like to admit. Sleep was never the primary concern as a teenager, but going to bed at 11:00 p.m and hoping that I'd be in good shape after waking up a mere four hours later would be a stretch for sure.

I laid my sleeping bag out on the questionable-looking area rug of his basement floor and tossed and turned for most of the time I was there. I wanted to be a good sport about it, though, and remained motivated to get out there and prove to myself that this would be worth my time. Counting sheep until I couldn't stand it anymore was my only option.

As far as I know, Sean slept fine.

At the crack of 3:00 a.m. Sean and I rolled out of bed (well, couch for him and floor for me). We geared up, sipped a half cup of coffee, and started the walk out. It was going to take a good while longer than it would if we rode the four-wheeler, but walking in quiet is well worth it. Most turkey hunters' first issue is having a bird see them while it's still in the roost, and I'm positive that nothing was looking for us this early. During our walk, we enjoyed the calmness of the morning air, stars in the sky, and hoots of your friendly neighborhood owl. To this day, these are all pretty cool experiences to take in. This was a good way to start the hunt. I was already feeling lucky.

We made it to our earlier chosen spots, surrounding the lower left corner of the field, looking back toward where we came. My butt hit the ground, and it couldn't have been much later than 4:00 a.m. I started to slowly realize there would be a lot of waiting ahead of me. From this time until 5:30 a.m. felt like hours... hours and hours, really. This was long before we had smartphones, so it's not like we could just sit and doom scroll into nothingness, turning our brains into mush until some action happened. I closed my eyes and did my best to be patient.

The first gobble sounded off as the birds in the roost were deciding what way to go. Now we were excited! *God, this is going to be good.* I couldn't contain myself. Sean was in charge of the calling, as I had never done that before. From time to time, I would hear him calling back and forth with the bird, not too much, of course, but it felt like the bird was talking to us. A big tom would be here any moment, and I'd have my chance! It was such a roller coaster ride to hear them go back and forth. We listened to the tom gobble for almost half an hour until I noticed some mechanical and unnatural-sounding noises.

At about 6:00 a.m., a truck came barreling over the hill, headlights blazing, and abruptly parked about fifty yards directly in front of us. I gestured to Sean with my hands as if to say, "I thought we were alone out here!?" (subtracting any expletives, of course). After a few bouts of pointing and hard looks, we decided that before this guy got comfortable, we would politely ask him to move his truck. We clicked our flashlights off first to try to get his attention without making too much noise—but he wasn't interested.

Quickly defeated, we had to come out of our carefully chosen hiding spots and march through the cut corn and leftover winter grasses, blowing our cover to any turkey in a one-hundred-yard radius. When we approached the man at the truck, he was getting his gear out of the rear seat. He was middle-aged and tall, but what I remember most is that he, at this point, was practically making an effort to ignore us. A grizzly bear could have been walking through the field, and his head still wouldn't have ever looked over his shoulder to see what was going on. I virtually had to tap him on the shoulder to get his attention away from his bow and arrow.

"Hey buddy,"

Sean was being too polite, but what the heck are two teenagers supposed to do?

"Didn't you see us over there?"

We explained our situation: the endless scouting, sitting here in the dark since four o'clock, me being a new hunter... and we asked if he would be so kind as to move his vehicle to a less noticeable location.

He quickly declined and announced, "Turkeys don't give a shit about a truck. Good luck boys." Slamming the door of the truck, he slung his bow around his shoulder and promptly marched off into the field, right up the game trail we were sitting by. He disappeared into the darkness of the morning forest, and we just stood there, completely stunned.

I had never wanted to shoot out the tires of anyone's truck before, but for the first time, I really did consider it.

"Some people are just dicks, and they act like they own the place... it happens." Sean tried to reassure me, but I think he was trying not to ruin it for himself, either.

We sat for an hour or so, restless as hell, never to hear a gobble again. I not only disliked turkey hunting now, as the bird was unattainable at this point, but now I hated turkey hunters. This new breed of assholes were just out for their own benefit, not willing to share the earth with any other human being. *Screw that guy*. To this day, I don't know who he was, but I hope he never even *saw* a turkey that morning. Honestly, I hope he never gets to see or shoot another turkey ever in his life! I hardly ever hold a grudge against anyone. I try to be a good person. But we were kids, man! This is a perfect example of why the sport of hunting needs more positive and supportive voices. After Sean and I walked out of the field that morning, it took me twelve years before I made another attempt to turkey hunt.

1.3 Disease

I absolutely hate that I am going to start a chapter with this. Let me apologize in advance.

Covid.

Yep, there it is. I feel like I'm ripping off a Band-Aid.

No one wants to hear about it anymore, but I have to start here. I have no choice. Because if it weren't for Covid-19 and the lockdowns, I would have never attempted hunting turkeys again, as I was perfectly content with forgoing another disappointment. The year 2020 was an absolute cluster, especially for me and those close to me. I was still a public school teacher, as were many of my friends, and my wife worked (as she still does) in the human services field. With that said, let me lay it all out, because this nasty little bug put quite a wrench in things and sent me searching for something new.

As my eyeballs were rolling up into the back of my head due to the boredom my students and I experienced from staring at each other through the computer screen, a few of my close friends, Jake and Todd, had an idea. They were teachers as well and needed to find ways, like all of us, to keep themselves entertained. After watching some episodes of Steven Rinella's show *MeatEater*, they proposed that we attempt a spring turkey hunt to break up the monotony of our current captivity. It's not like we were able to do anything else, so hiding away in the woods didn't sound like a bad way to kill time. Back then, I was recovering from an injury sustained while competitively running, and I was looking for a challenge that wouldn't beat me up too badly. I didn't know this then, but even though I'll never fully get back to "normal," my injury doesn't interfere much with the slow walking and stalking that hunting requires.

(Side note: Season ten, episode four, of *MeatEater* entitled "Flash in the Pan" also motivated us to do some flintlock hunting later in the year. I highly recommend the challenge for anyone into deer hunting. And, I'm sure you are already thinking about it, so no... I haven't killed a whitetail with that yet. It's no easy task.)

Jake and Todd are two of my closest friends and are always interested in anything out-of-doors. I have spent a lot of time with them outside, and anything from distance running to canoeing was on the menu. But with them, hunting was always the main course. Each could be considered a wild child in his own right. They are almost giddy in the woods, and I don't think I could name anyone more excited to experience nature than these two. They have big hearts that keep the people closest to them coming back, and they love to share the hunt with friends and family. At this point, I had been in the woods with them for the better part of the decade I spent as a teacher. I'd knocked more deer down with these two than probably anyone else besides my own dad and brother.

As far as hunting goes, we are always in the loop together on who is where and what is going on. Back then, it was exciting to try hunting something else with them for a change of pace. We organized some time we could get out together that May and planned a turkey hunt in the early stages of this new lockdown era.

My first turkey hunt with them is what got me addicted to pursuing this animal. I know you probably expect me to just sit here and start complaining about it, but honestly, this and the following hunts of the season were probably some of the most fun in my life. During this time, getting out of the house and doing something different was a very welcome break from our newly captive lifestyle. Lottery tickets and take-out food on the back porch were fun, but those things just didn't scratch the itch like trying a new hobby. Unlike said lottery tickets, hunting is a gamble worth taking.

We decided to meet at 5:00 a.m. on what turned out to be a cool morning that spring and walked in the dark up to a field that was part of Todd's property. (All of the turkey hunting extremists are probably judging me right now. I now know this was already way too late.) A local farmer grew crops there: a rotation of corn, soy beans, and hay. So, just from experience, we knew that birds came in semi-regularly to visit the field and areas around it to feed. A mix of crops, a large swamp with scattered hardwood trees, several small woodland ponds, and steep hillsides thick with fallen leaves have always made hunting there interesting and full of surprises. Patches of deep green hemlock trees were arrayed around the property as well, leaving a crisp freshness in the air that could only be experienced in Pennsylvania. Anyone who is out in the woods a lot experiences a great deal of unique nooks and crannies of the landscape, and this particular hunting area kept us on our toes throughout the years.

Our game plan was overly simple and looked like this: Walk quietly up to the field, listen for a turkey's gobble, walk that direction, and set up.

(Riveting, I know.)

But that's the best we rookies knew at the time, and at least we were all on the same page. Our plan started out pretty great. Once in the field, we listened for that first *thunder chicken* to break his silence and noticed gobbles coming from a hillside directly in front of us, probably five hundred yards out. *Not bad!* Jake, Todd, and I started marching that way, through the field, across a brushy old logging trail, and past the first small pond. We decided to set up in a line of pine trees where we could see the adjacent hillside and watch for any animals that might try to move down the path in front of us. They somehow determined that I was the best at calling turkeys. So, we spaced ourselves out at about fifty yards apart each, and I stayed the farthest back from the path, in an attempt to draw the bird in front of as many hunters as possible. Todd sat directly above me on the hill, and Jake, sitting where we imagined a bird would come to first, stationed himself just above Todd. We were all able to stay within eyesight of each other and felt that this area was well covered in the case that a turkey tried to sneak through.

Hunting wild turkey as an adult for the first time was such a different experience than it was as an eager teenager. I have had plenty of hunting experiences up to this point to help me plan for any unknowns that may come my way. In all honesty, as exciting as it was to go out, I wasn't hyped like I was as a young man. My mind started much calmer before the hunt as a twenty-nine-year-old than it did at seventeen. I slept well, felt good, got some hot black coffee in me, and as I sat down in that spot, I could absorb so much more of what was going on around me.

It's crazy to think that so many people have never sat in the woods early in the morning and watched the world come alive. They are missing one of the greatest experiences that I think we can have as humans. The birds wake up first and begin to sing, then the sun starts to peek over the horizon and fill the world with color. Soon after, you feel the warmth of the morning breeze on your carefully exposed face and hands as the temperature changes. It's so relaxing that it's no wonder so many turkey hunters lose out on killing a bird due to falling asleep up against a tree somewhere. Taking all this in only makes the gobbles of that first tom so much more enjoyable. There is a majesty that the turkey has as he calls down to the world, exclaiming that all he sees is his domain and his alone. I highly recommend giving it a try and experiencing it, hunter or not. Pick up a camera, put on some camouflage, and see what is out there to encounter. These early mornings won't disappoint.

Before this hunt, it was unbeknownst to me that calling a turkey too much can be a hunter's greatest downfall. Pro tip: call for the bird to tell it where you are, and then *shut the hell up* so he starts looking for you!

My rookie mistake practically included a full conversation:

He gobbled.

I called.

He gobbled again, and well, time to call!

Rinse, repeat.

I pulled out all the best calls I could. I tried the "Hey baby, how you doing?" and even, "Want to be my prom date?" He called back every time. I was sure he was telling me, "Hey girl, you're in for the ride of your life, and I'll be right over in my dad's new car."

Up the line, Jake and Todd gave me the thumbs-up as they were also convinced that this was going well. Calling continued until about 6:30 a.m., and as I have now learned, it's pretty typical for birds to quiet down after they remove themselves from the comforts of their roost and approach their target. The woods went silent, and my phone started blowing up:

Jake: Where did he go?
Todd: What did we do wrong?
Me: I had him! What's going on?

We had so many questions as the woods went silent, and vigorously debated through text messages if we should move to a new spot. We decided to stay put until about 7:00 a.m. This is also what we would now refer to as "about lunch time," since it feels like we have been awake for half a day already!

We sat quietly for the last half an hour and agreed to re-group. I now know that moving locations when turkey hunting is highly risky, and that almost never, unless there are no other options, should a hunter move if not absolutely sure. I walked to Todd first, then we walked to Jake, and to our surprise, a gobbler, fifteen yards in front of us, jumped up and flew away. This happened so fast, we didn't even know what to do! I stood there with my gun at my side and watched it disappear into the briars as if a train were crashing right before my eyes. I was frozen.

"Jake! How did you miss that?" The first few words out of Todd's mouth were nothing but a good ribbing. We were convinced he must have been asleep. Jake pleaded his case, swearing up and down he couldn't see that spot from a seated position, and just for the sport of it, we agreed not to believe him. (I mean, that's what friends are for. Right?)

I assure everyone, since then, I have sat in that spot many times and even observed where that turkey could have come from, and there is no way he could have ever seen it. These birds are smart; they have to avoid predators every day. They know how to move in the low areas and are aware of what natural cover hides them best. Countless times since that day, I have seen both male and female turkeys use various terrain to avoid predation and work the landscape, walking as silently as possible when need be. This ability of theirs challenges me even now, and I would like to think I know more than I did then.

We needed to do something different. Clearly, this spot was done for. Jake had to leave, so Todd and I were on our own. Directly above us on the hill was a large, half-moon-shaped depression of land that was covered in heavy brush and wild grape vines. We refer to areas like this as a "bowl," and hunters look for these in the landscape, as they often attract animals that are looking for a place to rest. There are hiding spots and food here, so we decided it was worth a shot. Todd and I headed that direction and hunted for another hour or so, sitting just off a four-wheeler path, before suppertime was upon us (8:30 a.m.). I made a few calls here and there in what felt like a futile attempt at enticing a passing gobbler to come check us out. I used a few new ones this time, offering a big tom his "first kiss" or just to come over for "Netflix and Chill."

The woods stayed silent.

That's okay, though, I thought. We had some action, and I wasn't disappointed with the morning activities. When our time was up, I gave Todd a wave, and we decided to get up to walk home... Immediately, I saw Todd's gun come to his shoulder. He tried to move for a shot, and in an instant, I saw him lower the shotgun back down. The disappointment on his face was immediately apparent.

"Two gobblers side by side," he said. "How didn't we see them?"

It's crazy to think that during my first time hunting turkey in twelve years, with absolutely no clue what I was doing, I set up three good birds in one morning. However, we learned an important lesson: move slowly and look around as much as possible before moving too far.

Todd and I enjoyed a good chat while leaving the woods, as we often do, each of us telling stories of what the kids were up to, who did this or that at work, or just pushing buttons to get a rise out of each other. It's our typical routine. This first hunt was a testament to what was to come that season, and we had a ton of fun as we called in birds, found great places to sit and hunt, hiked beautiful mountains and valleys, and all in all, saw over fifty different turkeys. Todd and I averaged three—sometimes four—mornings a week in the woods, with Jake jumping in as he was able to. These were some great memories to have with friends, and honestly, I owe it to Covid.

Weird, right?

The last day of that spring season, I convinced Todd to come out and give this turkey hunting thing one more shot. We sat in the woods all morning with zero action, and we were getting tired. As the morning passed us by, we decided it was time to head back to the fields. We did our usual chatting as we went along and followed a set of old logging roads that led into the farthest back corner of the fields. We made it through the first field and approached a line of tall hemlock trees used for a windbreak to protect crops.

"Stop, get down," Todd urgently whispered to me. "There are two birds at the top of the field and you're going to kill one."

Game time, baby.

We took a few minutes and came up with a plan.

As these two avian masterpieces unknowingly sat in the morning sunshine, we saw that the bird on the left was bearded. Not a wall hanger by any means, but I'd be happy to have it and have something to show for my countless hours of hunting. We decided that Todd would do a few soft calls in the back to keep the turkey's attention as I closed the gap to get in range of a shot. The turkeys were oblivious that we were there, and once I was confident of the position I was in, I lined up behind a tree. I waited patiently for the birds to come my way—a few steps in the right direction was all I needed—and I took my shot.

Bang! The gun went off, and I saw the bird roll through a cloud of dust. To my surprise, it immediately got back up, so I put another shot in it as quickly as I could. When the shot hit, the bird was off the ground, attempting to fly away. In what felt like slow motion, I watched the gobbler fall through the air upside down, wings open. It landed on the ground.

"Gobbie down!" I yelled back to Todd.

Or so I thought.

I turned to Todd, only to see him running up behind me as fast as he could.

"It's still moving!" he yelled. My heart sank deep into my chest, and I was caught off guard when I heard the loud crack of his shotgun go off. Now, it was a team effort, but our time had paid off. We shot a turkey, and at this point we were just proving to ourselves that this hunt was actually doable. Taking a bird home any way possible was icing on the cake.

After a few high fives, we turned back to where the bird was, only to see... nothing. No feathers, no blood, not a damn thing. This journey of disappointment began again. I shot my first bird, but now I suppose that I just turned it into coyote bait. All hunters lose an animal at some point in their careers, but man, did this one suck! How did I not see that bird get back up after Todd's shot? A whole season of work, waking up early and learning as I went, boiled down to only losing this bird. To date, in my life, I have only shot two animals that I was unable to recover, and it twists my guts up in knots just thinking about them.

After twenty minutes or more of searching the edges of the field for a sign, we called it quits that morning. I shot a target that we set up and wasn't super happy with my shotgun's pattern. So, convinced that the gun was the problem, I traded my old Winchester in on a brand new Mossberg the following week.

Grinning ear to ear when I put it in the gunsafe, I couldn't help but think, "I'll get 'em next year," and was quickly hit with, "Well, at least I hope I do."

No one wants to cause an animal pain. If anyone reading this book meets a hunter who does, tell them to seek help. *Seriously*. I think that anti-hunters sometimes believe that we are there for the detriment of an animal, but I know so many people who put conservation and ethical practices at the forefront of their experience. I personally hunt for the enjoyment of the outdoors and to reap the reward of some great meals afterward. Humans should do what they can to care for the animals they hunt, but we also need to remind ourselves that nature can be brutal. When a coyote or a bobcat kills a turkey, I would think that it would be more drawn out and horrific than what I did that morning. We would just call it the circle of life and move on. The bird I shot that morning probably didn't make it, but I doubt it was wasted in natural terms.

As a related side story, several years later, I bushwacked a big gobbler. I was walking down an old logging road on a local game land I frequented, which I refer to as "the green road." Logging crews planted it with grass down a steep section of the hillside to protect it from washout after their logging activities were done. It makes for a unique area to hunt, as the road passes through old clear cuts and off the side of the hill to a swampy creekbed.

On a mid-morning walk to find a better hunting spot, I turned the corner at the bottom of the road, and I could see a big bird strutting in the sun at the edge of the hill. Two other very impressed-looking turkeys stood right behind him. I knew he was a little far out, probably forty or fifty yards, but I had the new shotgun and felt confident. Time was limited before he saw me, so I quickly readied my shot, and when the time was right, I let him have it. The boom of the 3.5-inch magnum shotgun shell rang out through the hollow, and the turkey nonchalantly took a step back. He looked around for a second and immediately made a run for it. I unloaded two more shells in my haste—like a moron—and missed the bird completely each time. Some foul words followed, and my guts turned inside out. Here I was again, searching for something that felt impossible to obtain.

It's just a bird, how hard can this be?
Did I hit him?

I looked for almost an hour. I never found a feather.

When I got home that morning after a long hunt, I threw my hunting license in the garbage and called it a season. I was convinced for the next couple of hours that this was the last time I was going to hunt for turkeys. Looking back, I think I simply didn't have what it took to get the job done. A close friend of mine has said I am a good enough hunter, just not a patient enough hunter for turkeys. I didn't know that four years of hunting wasn't considered "patient," but he was right. When you're in the moment, turkey hunting requires a mental game I was not yet familiar with.

Turkeys have some mysterious power of slowing down time, and as the hunter, you have to be willing to roll with it. I talked with another local hunter who described a situation to me where he watched a big tom for three hours before it left his area and moved on to bigger and better things. He called it in, and the turkey walked around the perimeter of an entire field—just not on his side of the field. *Naturally*.

I had the good fortune of having a wife who assured me, and continues to assure me, that if you love something, you don't give up on it. It's crazy how we as humans are drawn back to things that interest us, even when we aren't the most successful at them. Many call it stubbornness, but striving to learn and grow runs deep in all of us, and we just have to find what scratches the itch. I look back at these experiences and see it as a testament to how tough these birds really are. I have talked to a bunch of different people about these specific instances. Some have assured me that I didn't hurt that first bird at all, with my shot being about forty yards out. My taxidermist said all I did was the equivalent of "hitting it with a tennis racket." On the other hand, I have a cousin who kills a turkey every year and claims that anyone could take a bird at forty yards with the right gear. Maybe a different choke, angle, or aiming for a different spot, and so on, plays much more into the success of the hunt than I would have initially thought. I'd have to say, though, when I see guys shooting birds with tiny .410 caliber shotguns, it makes me think I am much more of a novice at hunting birds than I would like to admit.

Regardless of the outcome of this first turkey hunting season, the unfortunate lockdown period of our history has given me more memories and stories than any other time in my hunting career. Anytime Todd, Jake, and I are in the woods together, we are always reminiscing and joking around. That's really what hunting is about at the end of the day, and for me, it's one of the good things that came out of the whole experience. I could pull out a hundred negatives from the early Covid days, but between that and my injury, turkey hunting was an amazing way to fill the void and keep my mind busy.

In all honesty, Covid did a lot of good in Pennsylvania for outdoor recreation. I saw more hunters in the woods, more people taking advantage of the trail systems we have, more involvement in the state parks, and the governor at the time even opened up trout season early for people to enjoy and get their kids out of the house. I think many of us learned some important lessons about what most viewed as entertainment. I can only hope that as we move farther and farther away from the whole experience, we don't forget about the natural resources that are all around us and what they have to offer.

Now, do me a favor, and get off of the pacifier—I mean—*phone*.

Go outside, enjoy the little things nature has to offer, and make some memories... You never know what you may find.

Part 2: The Birds Around Us

The Wild Turkey
Kingdom: | *Animalia*
Class: | *Aves*
Order: | *Galliformes*
Family: | *Phasianidae*
Subfamily: | *Meleagridinae*
Genus: | *Meleagris*
Species: | *Meleagris gallopavo*

I'm not writing this book for my own health. I want to tell stories and personal anecdotes about my hunting experiences, sure, but I'd like to also bring to light research on the turkey itself. Not taking the time to discuss the broad range that these birds inhabit in North America, their skill sets, and the species as a whole would be a crying shame. So, while some of this research is for the purpose of the book, the rest is to preserve my own sanity moving forward. I have definitely proved that I could use a little more information myself if I ever plan on shooting one of these blasted things.

The wild turkey is an adaptable and brave semi-flightless survival machine. No matter where someone lives in the United States and surrounding countries, they will find a turkey nearby. Probably because they are omnivores (eating a range of seeds, nuts, berries, small bugs, amphibians, and more), they are able to overcome environmental hardships and food shortages in the many different regions of North America. "*Be diverse in your approach to culinary delights*" is truly a lesson from this great creature. The turkey has also learned to evade the greatest hunters, bears, bobcats, eagles, owls, coyotes, and even, sometimes, *traffic*. They typically do this by sleeping in a roost at night, high up in the trees, and knowing the landscape around them. Turkey fossils have been found and dated to about five million years ago in North America, a testament to their adaptability. Turkeys have endured here for a long time, and they are masters of their own survival, as the bird we know today is virtually unchanged in regard to evolutionary standards. (No wonder I can't get one.)

There is a lot to do in a turkey's short lifespan of three to five years. Males (referred to as "jakes" when they are young—"toms" or "gobblers" once they reach sexual maturity) have to battle for rank to secure a group of hens for breeding. This is done by "strutting," where they puff themselves up and drag their wings on the ground in a grand display of masculinity and strength. They also have to fend off other potential suitors. The male turkey is equipped with long spurs at the bottom portion of his legs and will fight with other dominant males if they make a pass at his group of hens. Gobblers may also use these spurs to defend against predators (although they prefer to run away). If running isn't effective, as a last-ditch effort, the turkey will kick with its spurs to create cuts, scratches, and punctures against the likes of foxes, bobcats, and others. The spurs on an old bird can grow quite long, and this is one of the primary things that trophy hunters look for in a mature bird, although spurs are only second to the length of the gobbler's beard when it comes to bragging rights. Beards are a pronounced tuft of hair-like fibers that come in a strand at the center of a male turkey's chest. The longer the beard, the older the bird, and this is considered a key factor in a "trophy" animal.

Keep in mind, it's always better to harvest an older animal in almost any hunting situation, as they have less to offer to the gene pool later in life. Even though my primary goal of hunting is to procure food, when selecting a bird, given I ever have the chance, these factors will play into my choosing of a turkey to take from the flock.

Females, or "hens," have to rear and protect chicks, sitting on a nest for about twenty-eight days with little to protect them other than a keen eye and a defensive layer of about five to six thousand feathers. Females are social and can be found in groups of up to two hundred birds in the winter months. They engage in a unique social structure of leaders and followers. The ability to adapt in their vast numbers, as well as their smaller frames than the male turkey, makes females quick and razor-sharp in the woods when it comes to survival.

Only 21% of modern hunting license holders tackle turkey, and to me, this seems to be a surprisingly low percentage. After deciding to take on the challenge, these hunters (like all hunters, really) run into "handicaps" that are put in place, increasing the challenge of taking on a turkey hunt specifically. Both the individual and the state they are hunting in dictate this concept. These handicaps aren't meant to make the pursuit miserable, but are important conservation tools when controlling the population of a bird that was once decimated. Wild predators work with what they have, but we could tactically harvest an unknowing bird from a mile out with a .50 caliber rifle if it were legal and effective. It's not. If that were the case, we would end up in a historic buffalo-herd-type situation, where the birds could be eliminated so quickly, there would be no natural way for them to repopulate.

Recently, thanks to conservation efforts primarily beginning in the 1940's, there is currently a national population of about seven million turkeys. This number is made up of the total population of the five subspecies of wild turkey, and we are lucky to have them in this modern day. The Gould's and Osceola Wild Turkey took the worst hit due to poor animal management, and the other three—the Eastern, Marriam's, and Rio Grande Wild Turkey—reached dangerously low levels before there was (mostly) government intervention to add protections to their population. Each of these turkeys ranges in size, color, and vocals, as they are fine-tuned to the environments they call home. Turkeys contribute to the biodiversity of our forests and other habitats and are an essential part of the ecosystem, so it's our duty as hunters to be responsible in our approach to harvesting them.

As a ripple effect of poor management, game laws have developed, leading to our modern, successful turkey population. Each individual state puts its own limits on the hunt in terms of camouflage, caliber, or type of firearm to bear. Hunting each of the five subspecies of turkey that are in North America looks different depending on where you are geographically. Each of the fifty states may limit the time of the year people hunt turkey or the duration of that time in terms of hours. In Pennsylvania, for example, a shotgun can only be used with BBs no larger than four shot, and/or a bow and arrow with a broadhead of a minimum size of ⅞ of an inch. Here, we also have two seasons. The first is in the fall and the second is in the spring, the fall being more hunter-friendly, as you can take either a male or female bird, and the spring being more of a challenge, since you can only take a bearded bird. These hens and gobblers react differently to hunting tactics in each season, and each of the five subspecies has their own nuances of how they survive in their respective areas regarding food availability, opportunity for travel, and mating. There is a lot we as hunters have to keep in mind before marching out into the field.

Each state starts the management of the species with a baseline of hunting regulations. For example, the regulation of square inches of fluorescent orange clothing is probably the most nationally well-known game law. Then, hunters may choose to make it as hard or easy to pursue game as they see fit, depending on the level of success or challenge they are willing to undergo. Some hunters will only hunt in the mornings. Some hunters choose smaller caliber shotguns. Various other preferences come into play as well, such as only being willing to harvest a male bird. These choices can help manage turkeys in local areas more reasonably, as hunters know what is typically around them. Someone who scouts well can take a mental note of turkey activity in a specific area and get a feel for the local population, feed, and terrain.

I personally am more of a meat hunter than anything else. A good meal is a better motivator for me than nice antlers on a buck or an old long beard that is past his prime. So, as the predator in this situation, I haven't been picky about what turkey I am going after and have tried to make this as easy for myself as possible. I would like to just start with harvesting a turkey and go from there.

Each of us has a decision to make about how we approach the turkey's habitat, feeding habits, and routine. Many natural factors play into these decisions as someone makes adjustments in the field. Turkeys that frequent a low swampland may play a different game than turkeys in a hardwood-adorned mountain flush with acorns. My beloved birds in Pennsylvania would most definitely be a unique challenge to a hunter used to the birds that inhabit Florida or Kentucky, for example. (Although I can't prove that personally.)

My experience hunting turkey has been exclusively with the Eastern Wild Turkey, and they are, with no other way to describe it, a pain in my ass. Their population covers an extreme portion of the map in comparison to other subspecies. They are considered to be the most challenging of the five to hunt, despite being widespread on—this is a tough one—the East Coast (go figure). I imagine hunting them is such a challenge because of their sturdy combination of strong gobbles, stubbornness, and willpower. We'll dive into all that later on. As far as the other subspecies, I haven't had the opportunity to pursue them, but if I did, I'd probably just write a second book about not harvesting them on top of this one. Maybe I'll get rich one day and have the opportunity.

I think it's important for the purposes of this book to recognize the different turkeys that inhabit the land around us and take some time to think about what their little life looks like before interacting with them more. Hunting isn't just about bringing home dinner. It's also about making sure the next generation can as well. Conservation is a key factor for enjoying the outdoors long term, and the existence of these birds is important to the ecosystems and natural order of the regions they inhabit. I want to stress how important this concept is for hunters to understand, and I urge hunters to continually learn about the birds and their habitats. Understanding their food sources, what they are sources of food for, and how they navigate the landscape around them can help us keep an eye out for what resources we need to protect. Turkeys play an important role ecologically, and if we want to hunt them into our old ages, we have to keep nature in mind. In the following pages, I'll look into these turkeys' lives a little deeper, and maybe my research here will glean a little bit of insight for the next hunt.

2.1 Potential Danger

Troy slowly and methodically worked his way through the dark to find his well-scouted (and favorite) turkey hunting spot, deep in a state forest near central Pennsylvania. As a veteran turkey hunter of twenty-plus years, he could tell success was just a sunrise away. He knew turkeys often frequented the area he currently occupied, and so he found a spot and got comfortable. The dawn broke, turkeys gobbled, and Troy let out a few soft calls from the mouth call he used as he tried to coerce a big tom his way. He sat quietly after a few calls, knowing the gobblers would become curious and start searching in his direction, looking for a potential hen to call their mate.

It was a regular morning of hunting for Troy, who has been a friend of mine for a few years now and has no shortage of hunting stories to tell. A "retired" hunter, he traded in the woods for his enjoyment of other hobbies some time ago and now spends much of his time with friends and family. I've heard this story of his more than once, but it always stood out to me for how unique an experience it must have been. Once again, if a person spends a great deal of time dedicated to one avocation or another, they often get to experience the most exciting parts, such as my backpacking mink. Troy's story was no different.

He sat against the big tree he chose for the day and watched over a portion of the forest floor that was mainly open for animals to move about. Other parts of the nearby terrain were rocky, with slate-like stones off to his right side and directly behind him. To be successful hunting this area, his primary objective was to blend into this space and remain still, as the openness around him could give him away quickly to his prey. It was also an area that could be noisy, moving in and out, and that made it very easy for a turkey to pick out a potential predator. Despite the challenge, he had knocked down birds there before and knew what he was doing in this specific location.

After a short time, he could hear what he thought was a single turkey moving quietly behind him. Instead of immediately looking, he decided that it would be best to wait the bird out until it was as close as possible, then turn to shoot at the last second if he determined it to be a gobbler. Until then, all he had to do was continue to stay still. The animal's approach took a little time. Turkey don't always move fast, and they sure aren't on anyone else's schedule. Patiently and quietly, Troy listened to the soft crunch of footsteps creep across the leaves and into the rocks for about fifteen minutes. Now the bird should be in range, and his early morning hunt could be over long before brunch.

Deciding that the turkey was close enough, Troy brought his gun to his shoulder, swung to his right, and readied his shot. As he got his bearings, he realized he was now staring face-to-face with a red fox, not more than four feet from the end of his barrel! Once the fox realized that what it was looking at wasn't a turkey, it lost its balance, and a rock slipped out from under its foot. The fox fell with a crash and, spooked by the suspense of it all, hit the ground with a *thud*. Doing its best to avoid Troy, the red fox jumped straight up in the air, almost four feet high, in an attempt to change direction. It landed back on the ground in a panic, and with a shrill *yip*, it took off like a bat out of hell. The hunter had truly become the hunted, and Troy's morning in the woods, as short as it was, was over.

He laughs a lot when telling the story, and it's easy to tell he has fond memories of his hunting days. I am sure that the fox was planning on having a delightful breakfast that morning, and it was probably far more disappointed than Troy was about going birdless that morning. Oddly enough, of all the years that Troy had hunted turkey, this was the only account of predation from an animal that he had experienced.

I have spoken to only a handful of other turkey hunters who have had similar stories. Predation by a wild animal toward a human hunter happens only once in a blue moon, and it makes me wonder if turkeys are hunted by these same animals as hard as we would initially think. Sure, the turkey has plenty of regular predators, but are these predators going to consistently eat and hunt them? Or, do they just take the bird on opportunistically? For the laundry list of carnivorous animals that will eat turkey—anything from owls, to bears, to mountain lions—and for all the time we turkey hunters sit in the woods, calling and making noise, I can't believe I haven't personally seen more of these predators. I have been convinced for years that my turkey call should bring in coyotes as much as they do anything else, but maybe they are trying to track down easier prey.

There was only one instance during turkey hunting where I personally encountered a predator, and the instance was extremely brief at that. Early on in my turkey hunting career, the regulars and I would hunt the bird as if we were hunting deer, using the classic "walk and stalk" method of hunting. This is typical of Pennsylvania deer hunting, where instead of sitting in a treestand for eight hours straight, living on peanut butter sandwiches and freezing to death, the hunter will slowly work his or her way into areas that they know deer frequent. Then, using their intuition and listening skills, the hunter will take a brief sit in what they think is the best vantage point to watch for deer or other animals. This is done in increments of about one hundred to five hundred yards at a time, depending on the terrain or the hunter's fitness level. "Walk and stalk" is a great technique to hunt whitetail, but we quickly learned it is a terrible way to hunt turkey.

In these early years, we would move from area to area, getting a look around, scratching a call from time to time to see if we could hear or see a turkey that we could post up on. This was wildly unsuccessful, of course, but we live and we learn. Honestly, most of the time we were just glad to be out of the house.

After walking down an old logging road along the edge of a hay field, my buddies Todd, Jake, and I found ourselves in an area that had a low creek bed and tall pine trees.

"A bird has to be in here," Todd said. "Pistner, go down in the valley there and make a few calls." They stayed up on the logging road, and I slowly made my way down the valley to make a few calls and listen. After a few minutes, I looked up at them standing along the field road, to see that not twenty feet behind them was a young coyote staring right down at them! Its head poked right out of the tall grass. I could see the young predator's face and just past its front legs, as it only exposed itself enough to find out if lunch was downhill. I waved at them, jumped, pointed (suffered internally), and as expected, neither of them ever turned around to get a look. They were quite confused to say the least, and all I needed was for someone to look over their shoulder to see what I was trying to show them. I imagine the coyote quickly figured out we weren't the kinds of animals that should be making turkey noises. By the time I started getting too animated, he went off on his merry way, never to be seen again. I wasn't very happy with my friends, as killing a coyote would have been a rare treat that day. Harvesting a coyote is perfectly legal any time of year in Pennsylvania with a valid hunting license, but what could I do? I was the furthest away from it.

We have always joked that all our calling would produce a bear or coyote before a bird. I mean, why wouldn't it? And also, *what in tarnation* is a turkey hunter supposed to do if a bear sneaks up on them? I don't really have a good plan for what to do when some big black bear comes and sits in my lap. I have had countless deer come into my turkey calls and check out what all the fuss is about, but just not much in the way of predators through these short few years of hunting turkey.

Are turkeys that are preyed upon by natural predators hunted that heavily? My earlier question might need to be considered in a different way. Maybe it's not that they aren't hunted heavily or regularly, but that they are exceptional at avoiding predators altogether. Turkeys have three habits and adaptations which I think help solidify my theory that they do a better job of avoiding predators—and us hunters— than you would think. Because of them, maybe the predators have given up trying to make turkey their number one meal.

Only the strong survive, and in a turkey's case, once the jaws or talons of a creature prepared to kill it are clenched, I suppose there is not much else it can do. Turkeys don't have much in the way of self-defense, and the thick coat of feathers only goes so far when their head is bald and exposed. Their adaptations are primarily focused on escape.

The first adaptation a turkey has developed to avoid getting eaten is roosting. Sleeping high in a tree is a good way to get a solid night's rest and avoid predators. Around sunset, a group of turkeys can be found making their way to a thick bunch of high trees with low branches. They will climb high enough to avoid predation and get a good look around them. If a hunter finds a turkey roosted in the evening, and the turkey spots them, that bird will leave the roost in the morning, heading in the opposite direction to avoid the potential danger. Turkeys will do the same for any natural predator as well. This is why turkey hunters routinely wake up at absurdly early hours to pursue them. Sometimes, crow-calling will help hunters locate roosted birds. By doing this, the hunter can get turkeys to call them back without seeing them and avoid ruining the morning hunt. Birds will often "shock gobble" and answer to non-turkey noises, as if to alert others around them that a visitor, friend or foe, is nearby. Because of this, many hunters carry an actual crow call with them instead of just using their voice. Others will make a *hoot hoot* like an owl, but I don't recommend it, as it's my experience that turkeys identify owls as potential predators and may leave an area after their initial shock gobble.

The second adaptation the turkey has developed to avoid predation is their strong running ability. If a bird is caught off guard, the turkey far prefers running as opposed to flying. For a heavy bird like the turkey, flying is cumbersome and slow during takeoff. Their low and heavy frame makes it exceptionally difficult to get off the ground. Once in the air, a turkey can fly up to fifty-five miles an hour, but this is only under the right conditions. With strong legs and long toes and nails that allow them to grip the ground well, running at top speed happens quickly, and the ability to maneuver challenging terrain is a gift that is unmatched by other animals. Turkeys run much faster than humans do. A turkey can come off the line and, almost immediately, be up to twenty-five miles an hour on foot. Although their top speed isn't as impressive as that of other animals, including some of their predators, turkeys move so quickly that they can outpace a bear, for example, early on in the race. With their strong and powerful legs, these birds work their way through the brush, rocks, and swamps with impressive dexterity. Thus leading to their eventual escape.

A turkey's superb eyesight is the last of the three traits that keep them out of the clutches of a predator. If a hunter has a shiny button on their coat and is sitting in the sunshine, forget it. The turkey has spotted the button. This shiny object is unnatural in the environment, and *ol' Tom* has left the area long before the hunter has ever noticed. A turkey may lack a strong sense of smell and would definitely lose in a beauty contest, but it sees the world impressively better than we humans do. A turkey's brain is trained to spot movement from a great distance and can detect glares and shiny objects from afar. Not only this, but a turkey is also skeptical of everything it comes across that moves—big, small, or otherwise. Any prey animal is on the watchout at all times of the day, but the turkey is on another level. A turkey just watches the other birds flying around all willy-nilly whenever they feel like it, while they are mostly stuck on the ground. Seeing a predator before the predator sees them is a game-changer when it comes to survival.

Exactly how good is a turkey's eyesight?

I'm glad you asked.

We humans see about 180 degrees of the world around us at any given time with our fancy color vision and forward-facing eyes. Not bad for a predator. But when an animal is prey, they don't need to have eyes that focus on something specifically in front of them. Turkeys have eyes mounted farther apart on their skulls, giving them about 270 degrees of sight in their field of vision. This makes their eyes far superior to ours for finding out what is going on around them, and a turkey may see you long before you realize they're hanging out in your peripheral vision.

Hunting these birds is a real testament to a person's patience and comfort levels out in the woods. Turkey hunters have to be mentally and physically prepared to watch birds maneuver around them for extended periods of time. On top of that, we have to do this while we are making sure we don't give away our position as we scratch calls, wipe noses, or avoid the urge to send a text message to our lover at home. Being the predator in this situation and sitting still is harder than it may look.

I'm not a biologist (for God's sake, I'm not even a great turkey hunter), but it's reasonable to think that there are a lot of questions to be considered when it comes to the survival techniques of this animal. Are turkeys not hunted as much as we think they are? Or are they just good at not getting caught off guard? Maybe it's a bit of both, and I would think that most carnivorous birds and mammals are more opportunistic than we would initially think. An unsuspecting mouse or rabbit might yield a better success rate for predators than a turkey would, and predators may just be deterred from making a pass at these large birds. Regardless of which of the five species of turkey someone is chasing in North America, it's a fact that these birds have the right tools in their toolbox when it comes to survival, and they have had them longer than any unknowing hunter who has ever stepped foot into the woods.

2.2 Across the Rio Grande

Unfortunately, Reba wasn't singing about turkeys, so I won't take up any much-needed words on this page dissecting that song. Honestly, the whole title of this chapter is a little misleading, because I have no intentions of crossing the Rio Grande at all. Even though Mexico has a healthy population of turkeys, and with that, several different subspecies of them, I doubt many of the 21% of hunters taking on a turkey hunt have traveled beyond the border. It would be far too much tequila and heartache for this book if I start rambling on about getting snubbed in another country!

In the following chapters, we will just focus on the good old United States. It's enough of a challenge for us turkey hunters as it is, so why go beyond it? In the U.S, things are big, so naturally, we should start with the largest of the lower forty-eight states—Texas. And turning the focus to the largest population of turkey subspecies to inhabit it, the Rio Grande Wild Turkey. Although two other subspecies of turkey exist in Texas, this bird is the one people typically think of when someone speaks of the area. We can worry about the others later.

Taking up most of the central region of Texas, the Rio Grande Wild Turkey also historically spreads its wings into Oklahoma and Kansas, giving it a relatively large landmass to call home. These turkeys enjoy the more "rolling plains" type of regions that these particular states have to offer. In these ranges, the Rio typically eats grasses, bugs, and acorns. So, when scouting or hunting, look for habitats that sustain water and have ample food sources because of it. Other than humans, Rios enjoy the luxury of only a few predators throughout this area (outside of the ol' Wile E. Coyote).

As western expansion grew in the United States, hunters almost took the Rio Grande Wild Turkey right to the brink of extinction when over-hunting dropped the population in the 1800's down to about 100,000 animals. That sounds like a lot, but to put it in perspective, that is about how many people attend a Steelers football game each weekend in Pittsburgh. As we discuss other subspecies of turkey, you'll find this is a pretty regular trend. Hunters weren't regulated well at the time of America's western expansion. Travellers, armies, merchants, and hunters not only needed meat to feed their families, but in many cases would attempt to decimate populations for profit in the markets related to trade. The people responsible for our western expansion did this with more animals than just turkeys or buffalo, as history shows. Unfortunately, the destruction of animal populations was even purposely carried out to deter Native American populations from remaining in an area. (Yes, I'm trying to word that nicely.)

Thanks to conservation efforts starting around the year 1920, these birds are now at a sustainable level as far as population goes. Conservation groups have also spread Rios into other states, primarily in the western states, such as Oregon, but some birds are lucky enough to have been moved even as far as Hawaii. How awesome is that! Overall, these efforts have helped stabilize the population out of their core area and help promote hunting and turkey hunting in general. National numbers make for good statistics, but these birds have proven to do well in a variety of habitats that they may not have traveled to naturally. Their lack of ability to travel to places like these is most likely due to human development across the country that created literal roadblocks. Except for Hawaii, of course. I don't know for sure, but I haven't seen any research saying that turkeys are strong swimmers.

A Rio's current life isn't without hardship, though. Many of the young turkeys or "poults," as they are referred to, die or are killed off because of predation and the inability to roost up high when the bird is young.

Compared to other subspecies, Rios typically have lower success with their nests for many factors. Sleeping on the ground at an early age can make them an easy target for coyotes and the other predators that will selfishly look for an easy Thanksgiving dinner, regardless of the time of year. Also, these birds need about a six-mile range to call home and sufficient wooded areas within that for strong survival rates. Some biologists and researchers have shown that the Rio will migrate another ten miles outside of their usual range during the winter months to find better roosting areas. That's how important their range of habitat and food sourcing is for this bird. Southwestern landowners who graze cattle should take great care to prevent overgrazing and reduce cleared areas where these poults could be easily targeted by their predators. General property owners should make it a goal to preserve good fringe land masses around farms and residential areas with trees and brush, as these are spaces that the bird can easily call home.

As far as adults go, the Rio Grande Wild Turkey is a modest bird. They are the second-smallest of all five subspecies when it comes to most of their features. The beard, weight, and spurs tend to be more moderately sized in comparison with their avian brothers and sisters. Adult males weigh about twenty pounds, and females only average at twelve, putting them on the thinner side of turkey stature. Where these birds tend to stand out is their height. A male Rio, despite its weight, can stand top to toe at a whopping forty inches (most other birds are closer to forty-eight, but much heavier). These long and thin birds seem to be well adapted for the rolling plains' tall grasses and moving through them quickly while keeping their eye out for danger.

All turkeys gobble to communicate and win over a brood of hens for mating. The Rio's gobbles are a bit toned down in volume compared to other species, but they make up for it in aggressive vocal performances and personalities. Be sure to listen for their shorter crackling-sounding gobble when searching for a tom. Because of their aggressive calling nature and demeanor, it's possible that when hunting for a Rio, a hybrid bird will be seen or called in by hunters. It's not uncommon for a male Rio to breed with a hen of an overlapping species, as Rios will assert their dominance over willing hens and weaker males when they can. These mixed breeds don't seem to be recognized much by the hunting overlords because they don't have their own stable populations, but I am willing to bet that they are a pretty interesting animal to come across and harvest. If nothing else, it would be a great story to tell to family and friends.

Overall, Rios are beautiful. The tips of the tail feathers are tan colored, and the wings are adorned with a mixture of black and white feathers. The plumage on their bodies tends to have a chestnut color, while the skin on their legs is a very dark red. Anyone heading out to the south-central portion of the states looking to bag a bird would be proud to bring one of these home to the family. That's not just because it makes a great meal, but also because the bird is beautiful to observe. The Rio Grande Wild Turkey has a strong following of hunters and conservationists who are looking out for their habitat and well-being. Thankfully, this bird is now here to stay because of it.

The biggest challenge conservationists have moving forward with the growth of this bird's population is continually looking out for their habitats to encourage the success rates of the poults. It will be no easy task for them, but I think the bird will continue to endure. This lean and tough bird should be at the top of anyone's list, as it is an accessible and gorgeous creature. When planning a future hunt, you can expect to wear a lei in Hawaii or feel the wind blow the harsh arid Texas sand against your face. Either way, their place in our environment is second to none, and this bird is a true staple of the avian world.

2.3 The Gould Standard

Unlike the last one, this chapter title is no joke, so hang on tight.

The Gould's Wild Turkey is by far the rarest of all the subspecies in the United States and is only found in a small number of areas of Arizona and New Mexico. Starting with "big" as the theme in the last chapter, focusing on birds mainly in Texas, it only makes sense that we talk about the Gould's next. This is because the Gould's Wild Turkey is physically the largest of all the subspecies of turkey.

The Gould's is just like its counterpart, the Rio, in that it was almost completely wiped out by over-hunting in the late 1800's and early 1900's. (Go figure!) This required Theodore Roosevelt—a personal hero of mine—to step in with his conservation efforts of the time. Despite doing what he could, it was too late for the Gould's Wild Turkey, and the standing population of this bird was reduced to mere rubble. Conservation efforts continued well into the 1970s, but the population of birds in the United States continued to flatline due to illegal hunting, predation, and weak survival rates in poults. Remember, hens need large groups for survival, as well as plenty of space to call home, so poor land management and overhunting were probably two of the biggest human factors leading to the decline of the Gould's. These are factors that, of course, occurred outside of any legal hunting season. The poults of each generation were off to a bad start, to say the least, during this seventy-to-eighty-year span.

In the 1990s, a few conservation-minded men and women secured some birds from Mexico and made efforts to transplant thirty-five of them near their current North American locations. Because of them, we now get to enjoy a population of twelve hundred birds in the state of Arizona, and—wait for it—a whopping five hundred birds in New Mexico! Getting birds into New Mexico also required a transplant. Several years after the last transaction, Arizona traded sixty of its prized Gould's turkeys for a starter group of pronghorn and introduced them into areas where they thought the species would prosper. Just like children at recess trading baseball cards, the states found a more than creative solution to their animal problem. I am glad to hear that it worked out. Not only do I like to see turkeys do well in their native habitat, but I am sure that plenty of people (other than myself) would like to enjoy a healthy population of pronghorn to hunt for someday!

Even with these small population numbers on the rise, almost no modern hunters are able to pursue this bird, as they are very heavily regulated, and hunting occurs in very limited amounts. Most, if not all, hunts require the help of a professional outfitter. Annually, the tag for a Gould's is in extremely high demand, as hardcore turkey hunters look to complete their "grand slam" of each of the five subspecies. Hunting Gould's turkeys often comes with a hefty price tag because of their rarity, and it should. In an effort to raise money and promote a secure and healthy habitat, as well as continue conservation efforts for the bird, this hunt can cost upwards of five thousand dollars. A high price tag, but it's coupled with tax revenue subsidized by the sale of licenses, guns, ammo, and other hunting gear thanks to the Pittman-Robertson Act of 1937 [3]. This money generated can legally only be used to maintain game lands, state forests, and other approved conservation efforts throughout the U.S. Just another reason why I love these trophy hunters! Get out there and spend that money, boys and girls, because it keeps the cycle going!

Unfortunately, efforts to preserve the bird for future generations are hindered by continued illegal hunting. Both Arizona and New Mexico are working hard to save the populations that they have through the efforts of the state and multiple organizations. Not surprisingly, these turkeys also have to compete with other subspecies of turkey for resources in these areas, such as the Rio, and another turkey that inhabits these two states. Based on this information, I have a feeling that even if I ever do kill a turkey in my home state of Pennsylvania, I won't be committing to a hunt of the Gould's Wild Turkey anytime soon. This book is going to have to become a bestseller for me to fork out that kind of cash!

The ancestral location of these birds seems to have been first described around 1856 in the Sky Island area of southern Arizona and New Mexico, although currently, the majority of these birds live in the northwestern portion of Mexico itself. Little is known about them, but several key factors about their life have been determined through the studies of the bird we've managed since their recognition. For starters, they are birds that love the mountains. These birds can be found in the Animas, San Luis, and Peloncillo Mountain Ranges, roaming rocky and steep terrain between 4500 feet and 6500 feet above sea level. Talk about a hike! It is no easy task to get to habitats that they occupy, making them much harder to study than the other four subspecies.

Because of their location, Gould's turkeys are used to hot summers and mild winters. As the seasons turn to late spring and temperatures rise, Gould's turkeys begin their mating season, and hens raise their broods over the course of the summer. This consists of hiding the eggs unincubated for a highly secretive and secluded two weeks, then sitting on them for almost four more weeks after. After the chicks hatch, the hen spends about fourteen weeks raising the poults until they become independent and break off into their own social groups. Like all subspecies of turkey, these birds have their own social structure consisting of a dominant male and lesser dominant males below them. Research has shown that across all turkey species, this structure also gives way to habitat usage. The males that are most dominant tend to have the largest landmass to call their own, and lesser males take the leftovers. The stakes to get the best plot of land are pretty high, particularly in the case of this subspecies.

The size and characteristics of the Gould's Wild Turkey are as unique as the bird is rare. Again, this is the largest of all the subspecies; males tip the scales at a rather hefty thirty pounds! Females are only slightly larger than other turkey subspecies, coming in at fourteen pounds. Males gobble, but only at moderate rates, and tend to have only an average-length beard. I have seen birds in other subspecies with beards that literally drag on the ground, but for the Gould's, their beards only tend to sit right above the bare leg of the bird. Oddly enough, as large a creature as they are, with a body length up to forty-eight inches tall, the Gould's turkey averages the shortest spurs of all five subspecies. Overall, the bird is large and beautiful but has underwhelming "trophy animal" features in comparison to its other turkey counterparts.

When encountering one at first glance, the uneducated eye may think that it is a Rio Grande Wild Turkey. But the dead giveaway of the Gould's, outside of its sheer size, is the white tips on their tail feathers that rest against the darker feathers of their bodies. Long legs, tall frames, and the longest center tail feather of all the birds really set this beauty apart from the others. When the bird is as unique as this one is in comparison to the others, I would think that bragging about a beard or spur length after the hunt is almost completely irrelevant.

I may never get to go hunting for a Gould's; I don't think I could afford it. Monetarily or physically. But in all honesty, the idea of a "grand slam" doesn't entice me either, nor does any form of trophy hunting in general, so I'll rule this out early on. (I like meat more than mounts.) Regardless, for many, the cost isn't the important part of hunting this creature. Any hunter, hiker, or otherwise who ever finds themselves face to face with one of these majestic avian mysteries should take the time to appreciate their importance to the environment they live in. The attributes of a Gould's Wild Turkey are truly a testament to the diversity of these species of birds inhabiting our country. I'd love to meet someone who has had the opportunity to work with them or harvest one. The first thing I would ask them about is the story of how the hunt unfolded, as it's an ode to the efforts that hunters and conservationists have made in the last thirty-five years. I truly hope that this turkey is one for the ages, and that we get to enjoy it more and more as time goes on. If I were a betting man, I'd say Ben Franklin didn't know about these birds when he argued for the wild turkey to be the national bird in lieu of the bald eagle. But if he did, maybe a big, old, fat turkey would be on the dollar bill these days. By the way, I'm still holding strong that the Franklin myth is helping my argument here.

2.4 Midstate Majesty

Far more widespread than the last two turkeys, only one subspecies truly dominates the midwestern United States, and that is the Merriam's Wild Turkey. With that said, we now find ourselves wrapping up our journey through the core area I chose to begin with. The Midwest is extremely diverse, and turkeys not only take advantage of the vast and interesting habitats that this portion of our Nation has to offer, but also truly thrive there.

A bird that bears the name of famous biologist Clinton Hart Merriam, it was actually titled in his honor by a friend and colleague, Dr. E.W. Nelson, in the year 1900. Merriam was a busy man, studying several subjects and exploring much of the United States, but his focus for much of his biological research was nowhere near the likes of a turkey. His vocation was bears. More specifically, grizzly bears. Regardless of the naming process, it wasn't unusual for scientists and biologists to name animals after themselves or people they admired and worked with. Merriam, too, was generous when it came to naming his favorite critters, as he is the person credited with naming the "Roosevelt Elk" after his close friend, President Theodore Roosevelt.

Unlike the two previous birds featured in this book, the Merriam's Wild Turkey has typically had a healthy population across an extremely large landmass in the Midwest and western states. These "ditch chickens" (my wife came up with that one) can be found from Texas to North Dakota, and even all the way west into Oregon these days. This is mainly due to the transplantation of the species and the ample territory for them to roam in this area, allowing for their easy adaptation to different areas. Turkeys are absolutely unmatched when it comes to the range of environments they are able to prosper in.

Hunters often pursue this bird with ease because of their widespread habitats and the broad range of opportunities for multiple hunting license tags. This makes hunting them much more accessible and attractive to the average hunter looking to get a fresh turkey dinner, or just an excuse to get out in the woods for some rest and relaxation. Merriam's turkeys prefer mountainous regions of the Midwest, but can be found in the Great Plains and low swamplands as well. Like the birds before, they are versatile, omnivorous, and great survivors of predators. No specific terrain is a problem, and Merriam's turkeys make almost any area their home as long as there is a reasonable food source to be found. These turkeys have to avoid more predators in the wild than the other of the five subspecies, which makes them a real testament to their species' adaptability in different regions of North America. Many of these turkeys live their whole lives avoiding grizzly bears up north, while others live their entire lives without ever having to endure a grizzly at all in the south!

Why did I choose to equate this specific turkey with majesty? Well, getting a first look at the bird explains almost all we need to know here. Not only do they rule over the largest portion of the Midwest, integrating with many other subspecies of turkey across the board, but they are also a generally large and strong bird. Merriam's turkeys are noted for having a great mix of color across their bodies, including anything from deep blacks to blue and purple hues. Other than this unique coloration on their body, this turkey is most noted for two other major features on their plumage. First, both male and female birds have white speckling across their wings. When in a folded position, it can be easily seen, making a beautiful feather pattern across the side of their bodies. Second, the male bird has a mostly tan colored tail feather that is tipped in white, giving the bird a strong display when strutting. This large and bright group of feathers makes the bird easily visible to a potential mate. The Merriam's turkeys become quickly recognizable when compared to the other subspecies and have a particular uniqueness about them that the Rio lacks, the turkey with which it shares habitat the most.

Average-sized overall, male birds can stand in the neighborhood of four feet tall, weighing around twenty-four pounds, and females, who are always a little smaller, sit around the twelve-pound mark. When describing the bird, hunters and others familiar with the bird typically speak about their strong, muscular, dark red legs. The Merriam's turkey tends to have a bit more meat on its bones when it comes to its exposed legs, even though it has a below-average spur length, similar to the Gould's. The Merriam's beard is also typically small, which I personally find odd for the more robust bird that it is. As a hunter, I would imagine that these shortcomings wouldn't even be part of the consideration process when getting ready to bag a gobbler. The bird is so beautiful in full strut that the excitement of it all would be worthwhile in the end.

Also notable about them is that, for an extremely vocal bird, gobbling far more than any other subspecies and during almost any time of the day, they have an incredibly weak gobble. I suppose it's like being a bad singer in the car. Merriam's Wild Turkeys just like to listen to their own voice. When listening for their gobble, it could almost be described as the closest to what we hear from domesticated turkeys. Their call is short, with a few rolls, and just loud enough to get the point across. Merriam's turkeys can often be found walking and gobbling at the same time as they look for a mate or come into a hunters call. This trait of theirs makes them "the easiest" of all the turkeys to hunt. Some say that just not giving up on a gobbling tom will typically end with them coming into range of the hunter. Remember our previous lessons, and be sure to remain still and listen.

A family member of my wife's had traveled to Arizona a few years back to hunt for the Merriam's Wild Turkey. My wife comes from a mostly non-hunting family, and so even though I *love* to tell stories, they haven't spent time out in the field, so hearing about harvesting an animal doesn't really have the same gravity about it as those who are familiar. The first time I met this new (to me) cousin of hers, it was around Christmas time. I went into the basement with him to grab a beer, and my excitement went through the roof as I saw countless amounts of deer heads, bears, and birds arranged around the room. That's when I swooped in on my chance and told him I was a hunter myself. We exchanged some pleasantries, and he proceeded to tell me that most of his mounts were at a camp. The twenty or so animals I could see were just a small portion of what he had collected over his lifetime. Standing in the far corner, displayed in full strut, was a good-sized turkey, bold and colorful in a way that just didn't look like one of the birds around Pennsylvania that I was used to seeing. He told me that he had traveled to hunt, as he often did throughout his life, and one of his bucket list items was to bag a turkey out in the Midwest.

I enjoyed listening to his story of the hunt, which he described as "relatively easy." All he really did was wake up one beautiful morning in Arizona and call a bird in right after first light. *Bang!* The gun went off, and the next stop was breakfast. After I heard him tell this so nonchalantly, his story made me reckon with the fact that, unlike me, many people seem to think this turkey hunting thing is simple! I was excited for him, as I knew this bird was important to his hunting experiences, even though it came easily. His story really helped solidify the idea that hunters are proud of the time and dedication that it takes to get out in the woods and go after something they feel so fondly about. He told the stories of his hunts, not just to me, but also to hundreds of people in his life, and that is what makes this whole thing so great.

2.5 A Panhandle Hottie

This definitely isn't my area of expertise, but allow me to do a little bit of vacation planning here, as I have the trip of a lifetime mapped out. I happen to know how this goes.

The husband wants to go to Nashville. The wife wants to go to the beach. He wants to explore Glacier, Montana, and of course, she wants to go to the beach. Spouse number one is ready to hike the Appalachian Trail, and the other wants to go to the beach!

Again and again, many American families are struck with this dilemma.

Sound familiar?

Well, here is the compromise of a lifetime. The *only* place in the world that someone can hunt for the Osceola Wild Turkey is our lovely panhandle state—Florida. The powers-that-be should be marketing the idea that on a perfect vacation, someone can hunt turkeys while simultaneously their significant other can—go to the beach!

On second thought, honestly, I'm not sure how this would all go over. If someone's spouse did agree to allow them to hide in the Florida swamp for their whole vacation, searching for the elusive Osceola Wild Turkey, there is a good chance that they will be hanging out alone on the beach in their favorite swimsuit. Next thing you know, someone would end up trying to pick them up for a date. Marriages would be in more danger than that wild turkey ever could be! Although it would be fun to be a fly on the wall back at the Airbnb when that conversation starts, as I imagine that incident would rapidly change the vacation plans.

It's probably best to do this trip alone, but I digress.

On a more serious note, how awesome is it that the only place in the United States to hunt the beautiful Osceola Wild Turkey is in just a singular state? America is full of surprises around every twist and turn. Because of this specific turkey's confined location, it makes them an absolute rarity to most hunters and would require some extensive travel for many. Osceolas are described as a "hot commodity" among hardcore turkey hunters, as this bird is yet another challenge that stands in the way of completing the "grand slam" of each of the five subspecies. Once again, I don't personally understand to the fullest extent the idea of "trophy" hunting these days, but I will reiterate that I love these people! These selective hunters are traveling out of my area to hunt someone else's animals, upping my odds here at home. I'm filling the freezer without emptying my wallet, and they're keeping taxidermists in business all over the lower forty-eight. Sounds like a bargain to me!

At first glance, it would be easy to initially think that the Osceola may be a weak link due to its inability to move beyond the invisible border of the Florida-Georgia line. But rest assured that this incredibly strong and secretive bird has no shortcomings compared to its other subspecies counterparts. Although it is the smallest of all the wild turkeys, this hard-gobbling, and again, secretive avian soldier of the swamp has quite the attitude and has developed well for the part of the earth it inhabits.

It was W.E.D. Scott, an ornithologist, who dubbed the bird "Osceola" in the year 1890, after a well-known Seminole Indian Chief. The word "Osceola" could be boiled down to a simple translation of "shouter," which is, in my novice opinion, a very reasonable name to give to any wild turkey. The Osceola Wild Turkey is well-known for its incredibly strong gobbles, and yet, it is picky in what it answers to. These birds are often thought of as the absolute hardest to hunt out of all the subspecies because of this trait. Weak or inexperienced callers will surely spoil the hunt early on, so practice calling often before tackling this bird.

A small and very dark-complected bird with a plumage of blue and purple tones all throughout its body makes it incredibly unique. The Osceola is also adorned with brown tips on the tail feathers, which, unlike the Gould's or Merriam's white tips, make it more similar to its other subspecies counterparts.

Osceolas are also much lighter in weight than the other turkeys in North America. Males only weigh between fifteen and twenty pounds on average, and their female equivalent only tips the scales between eight and twelve pounds. That's hardly a dinner plate as far as I'm concerned, but, *gosh darn it*, it's more turkey than I currently have. Their longer-than-usual legs harbor the longest spurs of any of the subspecies, and they sure as hell need them. These turkeys have to avoid all the predators of the Everglades, including, but not limited to, panthers, bobcats, bears, foxes, coyotes, snakes, and—probably—alligators. Let's just say it doesn't hurt to play a little defense in this part of the country.

The modern-day head count of these turkeys is lower than that of many of the other subspecies. Although it's a highly challenging animal to track down, scientists think there are only a solid one hundred thousand in the state. That's not very many, but then these birds have had to compete with not only their natural predators in their lifetime, but were also hunted by humans far too heavily in the late 1800's. I reiterate *again*, before conservation was ever thought about and the grocery stores were much less abundant, many people toed the line between selfish irresponsibility and getting just what they needed. The hunting pressure at this time, coupled with the overharvesting of timber in the state of Florida, made it hard for the birds to roost, especially at a young age. When a turkey can't roost in a safe place or have access to hardwood trees with lower-hanging branches for them to climb, it makes it virtually impossible to avoid predators while sleeping. This gave way to lowered numbers of surviving poults, making it hard for turkeys to maintain overall population numbers.

Florida made major efforts to bring the bird back in the 1940's and again in the 1970's, with little payoff until the last twenty-five years or so. Although it is illegal to hunt there, Everglades National Park now has a thriving population of about two thousand birds since 2006, thanks to transplanting efforts and heavy scientific observation of the flock. This is a nice bolstering number for the state's population. By keeping a close eye on these birds in a regulated area like this, the scientific community is able to learn more about them.

Anyone taking on the challenge of hunting these birds should keep some of the above information in the back of their mind. Also, be sure to check on where and how the laws dictate the hunt of Osceola specifically. In most of the state of Florida, a hunter is allowed to take two birds per season, but it only takes a quick look at harvest reports to reveal that these birds present an adequate challenge. Most challengers of the Osceola are unsuccessful. Even though they can choose to pursue the bird by way of archery, shotgun, or muzzleloader in most zones, the problem will always be getting a bird in range. Most hunters, I would imagine, hope to just see some of these birds up close in the season, let alone pull the trigger on one. Tags are usually distributed by quotas, set for a certain zone or limited entry, so be diligent and get an application out there quickly if you need one of these birds to complete the elusive "grand slam." Out-of-state residents need to do their homework and get signed up for a tag double-quick, as they are almost as hard to come by as the bird itself.

While this is by far one of my favorite-looking birds, this small, strong gobbler will put a hunter at their wits' end and then have them coming back for more next year. It goes without saying that Florida has an incredible natural resource, as the Osceola is probably more rare than gold, silver, or oil. Until researching the birds for this book, I was guilty of lacking appreciation for how interesting and challenging the hunt for this turkey really was. And, I believe without question that anyone who gets to take on this hunt is truly lucky to share a piece of earth with the bird that calls it home.

2.6 Sworn Enemies

Finally, we have made it.

Here we are, at my beloved but frustrating Eastern Wild Turkey. The Eastern is the final of the five subspecies found in the United States. This is the bird that has eluded me for the past four years, created countless hunting stories, and has driven my wife and family into madness with my relentless pursuit of this plausibly mythical creature. I joke with friends and family that the hunt is personal at this point, and the bird is now my sworn enemy. The Eastern is truly awe-inspiring, and could break the heart of any man or woman who attempts to hunt and harvest it. This bird has caused me so much grief that if I were a pilgrim, it would have made sure that I would never celebrate a single roasted turkey dinner at Thanksgiving for as long as I lived.

The Eastern Wild Turkey is the most widespread of all the turkey subspecies, ranging as far northeast as the

New England states, as far south as Florida, and as far west as Kansas. Some of the birds have even made their way naturally farther north into Canada, but who needs them anyway? (Just kidding, Canada.) People have also been transplanting Easterns as far west as Washington state since 1913, and the turkeys have had a sustainable population there since the 1960s. It is no wonder that statistically, this is the bird I am after, as they take up the largest portion of the U.S. map. This reason arguably makes them (to me at least) the ultimate surviving machine of the five turkey subspecies. Eastern Wild Turkeys are able to tackle almost any territory, avoid any predator, and adapt their cuisine choices to whatever the landscape has to offer them.

Not only is it an absolute force to be reckoned with during the hunt, but the Eastern is also as beautiful as it is tough. One of the largest of all the turkey subspecies, adult males can weigh as much as thirty pounds, while their female counterparts stay around the average hen size of twelve pounds. These birds are adorned with white and black barred feathers on their wings and a chestnut-brown colored tail feather with dark black striping. The tip of the feather ends with a small row of chestnut-brown coloring. This color pattern helps them conceal nicely behind the sprouting brush and leaves of spring that they will often call home, and it's the perfect camouflage for the Pennsylvania forest. As with many other predators of the forest, be sure to see them before they see you! This is no easy task, and many hunters would never know that this bird was within range of their shotgun if they had not watched with a careful eye. Spotting this bird often takes a good bit of practice, and learning what to watch for can be a learning curve. The way they move about the landscape is very different from larger game like deer or bears.

The Eastern Wild Turkey is also the bird with the largest beard. Often, older males can have a beard that is so long it drags along the ground as the bird travels on foot. Many hunters of the Eastern want to know the beard length of a bird that their buddies have harvested, and these birds are often defined as a trophy when a beard is ten inches or more. I have seen multiple birds, at a distance of course, that had beards this length or longer.

Older turkeys seem to develop strong coloration in their head as well. I swear, sometimes in the spring when they are mating, the colors of their bald head are so strong, with so much red and blue in the skin and white tucked into the barred feathers, I think they had to be the inspiration for the American flag. These impressive features of the Eastern make every hunt a true trophy hunt.

These birds really hold up to the nickname "thunder chicken," as they have the strongest gobbles out of all the subspecies when it comes to calling in a mate. The booming gobbles produced by a senior tom are only matched by those of the Osceola, and when an Eastern is in full strut, they will relentlessly gobble while parading through an open field or clear-cut. Birds can often be heard from hundreds of yards away, and they can be difficult to locate when the sound is traveling through long valleys or across hillsides. Their heavy weight, strong gobbles, and build (slightly larger than forty-eight inches in total length) rounds this bird out as a real contender in the turkey world. Only the Gould's or Merriam's would closely match the Eastern in stature. Although these birds don't come close in comparison to spur length. Easterns also have long, aggressive spurs that can reach lengths of over an inch. I have even seen old birds that have spurs so long they start to hook downward, making them a useful tool for fending off their competitors during the mating season.

The diet of the Eastern is also impressive, as it allows them to adapt to the widely different landscapes they live in across the country. As poults, they feed mostly on proteins, eating small bugs and anything else they can get their beaks on in the early stages of development. As they grow older, most birds still eat a variety of bugs, but add plenty of vegetation, succulent greens, and other mast to their diet. In adulthood, they feed on mostly mast items they find opportunistically, such as berries, acorns, and plant seeds. Being well-rounded is important for hens, especially when they sit on their eggs in the late spring, as the only time they will leave the nest is to feed. So, it's important that they can grab food and return to the nest as quickly as possible to protect and warm the eggs.

Want to know what makes them so hard to hunt?

This isn't like deer hunting, where a hunter needs to be continuously washing clothes, neutralizing human scent, and hiding high in a treestand.

Oh no.

This is much, much more complicated than that.

An adult Eastern Wild Turkey almost has a three hundred degree field of vision when they are sitting still and can encompass the full three hundred and sixty degrees by simply turning its head. When someone hears the phrase "head on a swivel," this is as close as it can get.

A shiny button on a favorite hunting jacket? The turkey saw that. Can't help but wipe your face and clean off those cold spring morning boogers? Yeah, the turkey saw that too.

These birds are tuned into just the slightest movements and nuances of the woods. And it's not just the Eastern. All of the subspecies will "get out of Dodge" as soon as they think something is out of place, long before anyone knows they were there. Stillness is the only safe place for a hunter when sharing the woods with a wild turkey. By the way, turkeys are hunted from the ground, so be sure to find a good tree to lean up against, because you're going to be there for a while.

Easterns, along with the other subspecies, also have incredible hearing, way outside of our own human range of perception. Studies have shown that turkeys are able to hear into the subsonic and even supersonic ranges of sound. People joke about having too many voices in their head already, and we might be lucky that we don't hear what they hear. Every crunching leaf, every sneeze, and each broken stick rings like a fire alarm for these birds, telling them that danger is near. Anyone who has ever hunted the Eastern knows that they have an incredible knack for pinpointing the location of sounds. Because of their acute senses, calling for these birds is a close second to the Osceola when it comes to ranking the challenge of the hunt. My wife just *loves* it when I practice the slate call in the basement—but practice makes perfect!

The population of the Eastern Wild Turkey is now stable and doing well, but like all of the turkeys discussed here, the Pennsylvania Easterns had their trouble in the late 1800's and into the early 1900's when rapidly changing territory due to the overlogging of the state's forests put these birds down to a measly thirty-five hundred animals.

New game laws and an intense breeding program, put on by the game commission, brought the turkey back to life and created a more than healthy number for the state. These turkeys now take full advantage of the vast areas that Pennsylvania has to offer, and each flock can be found covering sometimes multiple thousands of acres of land. These land masses they call home are a mixture of game land (public land), state and national forest, and, of course, vast private lands. Landowners in these large private areas need to carefully consider how they manage their land and avoid removing mast-producing growth, like grapes and berries, which are an important food source for Easterns, as well as other turkey subspecies. The preservation of large hardwood trees that turkeys could roost in is also a necessity to the birds' well-being. A typical flock of Easterns is about forty birds, so landowners looking to develop an area should be considerate of the large habitat that turkeys need to be successful. If good care is taken by landowners, hunters, and concerned citizens, I have no doubt that the Eastern Wild Turkey will be here to stay—and torment me—for many years to come.

It really is a recurring theme in our human history that overlogging and poor land management have contributed the most to the downfall of this animal and many others. I am always sad to see a hen in the summer scooting through the woods with only two or three poults behind her, when in a perfect world, the number should be much closer to nine or ten. If this book has done nothing else at this point in the reading, I hope it creates a little awareness of how delicate animal populations are and how we really need to do better with our everyday conservation of land and habitat. Pennsylvania is the most forested state in the lower forty-eight and number two in headwaters, second only to Alaska. How in the world is it that, these days, a brood of birds has less than a fifty-percent survival rate?

I love loggers, farmers, factories, and the average red-blooded American citizen, because we all play an important role. But *do* better, people! We should ask others to be responsible for their land, too. If not, there will never be a chance to enjoy Mother Nature to the fullest capacity. Without the preservation of clean water, vast and diverse landscapes, and an animal's general room to roam around the county, the turkey populations we know now will quickly disappear, and there will never be another turkey hunt in sight for this poor old author.

Part 3: Hunting the Elusive Turkey

At this point in the book, you are probably anticipating that I will take some time to lay out the more technical details about hunting turkey.

It's expected, really.

I've presented my hunting background and stories and even provided enough research to hopefully look like a capable author (and maybe even a *real* turkey hunter). But it's hard to say.

As an avid hunter, many of my personal trips into the woods, regardless of what I am hunting, require similar preparations: finding ammo, picking clothes, practicing some shooting, scouting out a starting place, and much more. For many members of the hunting community, this preparation is just a regular part of life, as we see these acts as a necessity to our being. Most, if not all, outdoorsmen and women have their personal preferences on how they like to get ready for the hunt. Many non-hunters could probably relate in other ways to the specifics of our routines, similar to how someone might regularly go to the gym after work to blow off steam or jam to their favorite playlist while cleaning the house. There are just things that make it feel right.

Preparing for a turkey hunt is as much mental as it is physical. Many turkey hunters, especially in the New England states, do not have the luxury of just walking out into the nearest local farm field. Hunters in these regions pursuing the *elusive* Eastern Wild Turkey have to hike into the forest, sometimes miles at a time, to sit on some uncomfortable-as-hell hillside for hours at a clip. There have been countless instances where I have been two miles from where I parked my truck and have come across another hunter entering or exiting their preferred area for hunting. Apparently, I'm not the only one up for a good morning hike. It doesn't bother me, though; these people always make for some good conversations. Usually, my previous training as a public school teacher will quickly kick in, and I'll try to get some voluntary details whenever I run into another hunter this far out. I refer to these people as "the crazies," and they love to spill the beans on their morning hunts.

"Have you heard any birds this morning?"

"Have you been here before?"

"Where are you headed? I sure don't want to spook any of the birds you scouted."

These are my usual pleasantries anyway, while I'm really probing for knowledge—like any good teacher would. This is the gateway drug to get my new acquaintance talking and to start filling me in with the info I'm hoping for. I never want to spoil another's hunt, but I do want to know as much about it and the area as possible. Each hunter is a unique well of knowledge, and I want to get a drink of the water, even if it's low-quality water (a.k.a. intel). Knowledge and physical prowess are important when it comes to taking down a bird in the mountains. And for me, acquiring knowledge is becoming more urgent as my physical attributes fade, especially when I have to go that far out of my way for a good hint.

Through routines of my own, hunting with friends and family, and meeting others out in the field, I have narrowed down a few key ideas to consider. Maybe each of these upcoming subjects could be used in other aspects of hunting. But when it comes to turkey hunting, the brave who attempt it need to be ready for some up-close-and-personal encounters. Being fully aware of your own personal physical limitations and comfortable with your gear will change the game. In terms of how someone approaches the noble endeavor of turkey hunting, these are probably the two most key limitations hunters have. My personal inventory has changed rapidly over the years as I have learned from others and experimented extensively on my own, sometimes leading to my own detriment.

So now comes the part where I share some of my field findings and said experiments. Whether anyone decides to take my word for it—or not—is up to them.

3.1 Calling for the Big One

I once lived next door to the home of a somewhat well-known Pennsylvania turkey call builder and calling pioneer. People who know me in my local area would know the name without much detail beyond that. I even once had the pleasure of seeing the small shop where he created his calls. Not that it made me any better at calling birds. (I'm already finding this section laughable. An aspiring *turkey killer* writing a chapter on how to call in turkeys he has never killed...)

Through some of the chapters, I have briefly mentioned calling methods, but I would like to reiterate one of the most important lessons in calling that might ever be: *The hunter should always call less than they think they need to, and when the gobbler gets close, shut the hell up and make him look for you!* A turkey hunter has to view themselves as being hunted by the gobbler. In this instance, when calling, hunters need to portray the role of an available hen and act the part. Be interesting! Every successful hunter I have ever talked to tells me the same thing. It's like clockwork. I'll tell my hunting story from the morning to a buddy or family member and explain that the bird never came in range, went into full strut, and wandered around for a while, yadda yadda yadda.

Then they'll say, "You call too much."

Keep a few things in mind on the next trip into the woods. First, being a poor caller means a lot of body movement. Practice hiding your hands. Birds see everything, so yes, they see hands moving, no matter how well we think we hide them. Second, calling too much can make other hens jealous, and there is a good chance they will want to lead their gobbler away from this new and exciting potential girlfriend out yonder. Third, when a gobbler comes in, he will move back and forth in front of the area he thinks his potential hen is in, in kind of a half-moon type pattern: back and forth, back and forth. He does this to try to see everything, spot predators, and keep himself under cover until he is ready to come out and strut his stuff. Don't be foolish out there in the field. Animals can be curious, and curiosity kills the cat ...sometimes. Wait the bird out and let him play his game before considering a longer-than-necessary shot and rolling the dice on a botched hunt.

Types of calls and choosing the right one for you can be incredibly important. When I think of calling a turkey, I typically think of three different styles of calls. Many types of calls exist, but the ones I have chosen to write about I personally have experience with, and have seen implemented the most by other hunters. Each of these require their own fair amount of practice and technique, but some are easier than others to master. The first of these, by far the most iconic, is what we all know as the box call. Typically made of hardwoods such as cherry, hickory, or oak, the box call can come in a multitude of sizes and shapes. Box calls are built in the shape of what woodworkers would refer to as a "dovetail," where the profile would fit a ten-degree "V" shape if viewing it from the end, down the longest side. A screw and spring hold a paddle over the top with a hollow center below, allowing the edge boards to vibrate as the paddle is dragged across it. With this handy call, well-practiced woodsmen can get a wide range of *putts, purrs, kee-kees*, and plenty more, imitating the vocals of an available hen.

Experienced callers will even fashion larger box calls with a rubber band and shake the call vigorously to create a faux gobble that can trigger a tom to shock gobble back. This can be insanely helpful in locating a bird before accidentally bumping into one when changing positions in the field. The major downfall here with box calls is that the novice hunter has a high amount of hand movement. So learning to hide that movement can come with quite a curve. However, these calls have proven again and again to be extremely effective, so they are still the top choice of many hunters, both new and old.

I was a woodshop teacher for a short tenure of ten years. I'll speak from experience that if anyone ever needs to keep a bunch of teenage boys busy and doesn't mind getting some strongly worded emails afterwards from their coworkers teaching other, quieter subjects, this makes for an entertaining project. If anyone is attempting to make one on their own, don't settle for prototype number one. Experiment with different species of lumber, paddle shapes and sizes, and box length and width. There are many iterations out there and probably more worth exploring. Even change the angle of the dovetail, just for fun. Nowhere in the Bible does it say the dovetail has to be ten degrees, but some woodworkers would be willing to strongly debate that it could be listed as an eleventh commandment. The only thing you need is a few pieces of scrap wood to play around with and a couple of saws and drills. Electricity is even optional, as we live in the golden age of hand tools, so I highly recommend the attempt. Plus, I imagine that calling a bird in with a homemade call would be *very* satisfying.

Anyhow, my preferred call, believe it or not, is not the box call, even though I have made half a dozen of them on my own time and countless others with students. My call of choice is what is referred to as a slate call. A small wooden or plastic box holds a piece of slate stone inside that essentially gets "scratched" by what is essentially a stick (called the "peg") that you hold in your other hand. I like this one because it gets wet and quits working, and sometimes, if I'm extra lucky, one half of it falls out of my pocket, and I get to have a scavenger hunt while sitting in the brush somewhere. Fun! I'm already talking myself out of this choice, but I just love all the free entertainment!

In all seriousness, though, this call can give hunters a lot of versatility as far as the sound of the call. Sometimes, I sit in the woods and try to mimic the calls and vocalizations of other hens that I hear passing by. Over time, my slate has come to sound more dynamic and carries more "voices" in it than I would ever be able to get with a box call. My wife loves it when I fire up a few calls from the basement of the house, as I mentioned before, but it doesn't hurt to shake the rust off before the season starts. Or, in some of the in-between months, too.

Like the box call, hand movement is also a problem here, so I try to block the so-called "scratching" by sitting in a slouched position and hiding my hands behind my knees. I scratch in different patterns as well, not just straight lines or circles. The best sound I get is when I move in a "J" shape across different parts of the slate. With this technique and over time, many birds have been curious about me. I just tend to overcall, and they don't get close enough. I took a few desperate cracks at them in the past, but that sub-twenty-yard shot still hasn't presented its opportunity. Maybe it's me, but I feel better and better about using this call every time. However, I have spoken with some friends who love it and others who hate it, so I would recommend just trying it out before taking my recommendation and getting too invested in the slate.

Lastly, what seems to be everyone's favorite: the mouth call. This call works just like the reed in a clarinet or saxophone, by having a thin plastic diaphragm vibrate in between the two outer casings. The hunter should put it in their mouth, just above the tongue, let it soak a little bit to soften the reed, and then *apparently* make some hands-free noise with it by blowing across the instrument.

Or, at least that's what they tell me.

I've heard all the advice. I was told that I should just hold my tongue up against it to keep it in place between my teeth. *Or, was that right?* No, I should keep it on the roof of my mouth, just behind my teeth. But then I can't keep it "right behind my teeth," and it slides out unexpectedly. Nothing to worry about, the floor adds a lot of flavor, thankfully.

Want my honest but unpopular opinion about these calls?

They're garbage!

I have never gotten this stupid thing to work beyond some horrible squeak, and for whatever reason, I can't figure it out! (I was even in the band in middle school, and I thought I had a leg up on this one.) So, I am going to do the same thing with this chapter that I have done with the mouth call. Give up!

Good luck, and maybe just stick to the first two.

3.2 Hiding is an Art Form

Before I get too invested here, let us all just take a quick minute to appreciate the lack of effort our forefathers put into camouflaging themselves—*and* they still had complete success hunting and harvesting animals. Nowadays, if someone walked out in the woods with a rabbit fur cap, plaid jacket, and some beat-up old jeans, the modern hunter, in a new high-tech suit that just cost them seven hundred dollars, would laugh that guy right out of the woods. (Based on a quick search, seven hundred is probably low, depending on the brand.) How did the hunters of old do so well? Honestly, when I think about it, it's not too far beyond common sense when considering what an animal is looking for. This is, of course, in terms of what they designate as a potential predator.

Does someone need to spend a ton of money on fancy camouflage? No way! Would I also recommend that plaid option during these modern times? Still the answer is "No."

The reason plaid worked well is because when hunters or animals are out in the woods, the most important thing they can do as a predator is break up the natural shape of their body with a pattern. Animals, including birds, typically don't see color the way humans do. Their vision is traded off to see better in the dusk and dawn settings when they are more active. So, color doesn't matter as much to them as we might think (or apparently overthink) as humans. Stripes, spots, zig zags, or *whatever*, all hide the shape of the animal's body when they are out in their habitat. Having a mix of patterns doesn't hurt too much either. Think about how animals naturally camouflage themselves in all regions of the world: zebras, tigers, cheetahs, etc., and then this concept doesn't start to sound too far-fetched. I have shot more deer dressed up looking like the great pumpkin than I probably ever have, or ever will, in full camouflage. The same could probably be said for the number of people in history who have shot a turkey in average work clothes versus the expensive stuff. Going out in the woods dressed in plaid, dark colors, or old jeans is probably just a hazard at this point. Modern hunting tactics see safety in one of two ways: completely camouflage so you can't ever be seen, or blaze orange to the max so everyone sees you. If you're in between these two ideologies of hunting safety, you're probably running the risk of getting mistaken for a game animal. It unfortunately happens more often than you might expect.

So... the average bear is on a budget, and they need some camo gear for turkey season.

What should they look for?

Here is my advice: avoid anything and everything shiny! If there is a button on the collar that can reflect light—cut it off and toss it in the garbage! If there is a fancy emblem on the sleeve—trash! If the company loves their logo and pastes it on with pride—chop it off! Essentially, if it catches the eye of the person picking it out on the shelf, it will for sure catch the eye of the elusive wild turkey. Common sense tells us that there isn't anything naturally occurring that is reflective in the mountains of Pennsylvania any more than there would be in the plains of Texas. So why do companies do it?

Must be because they are proud, and we as people love to pick a side. Hollister or Aeropostale? Nike or Adidas? Democrat or Republican? (Aww... I know, that one hit a little harder.) It's really the same question as Mossy Oak versus Sitka; it's all just camouflage.

"Who cares what they do or how they do it, that's the brand I want!" proclaims the moron. Simplify the problem, and find something that covers your body well and keeps the attention off you while out in the field.

I personally wear a cost-effective suit, something that has pants that match the jacket and a hood, and then

I just toss on some gloves to hide my skin. My boots are waterproof, and a light hat to keep it interesting rounds it off. A face mask is recommended, but only for the brave. It can be hard to tolerate, so keep it light. I just recycle my gator from deer season year after year, because I forget to get a new one in time, and I don't recommend it. These are way too warm, buy a mask that fits well and keeps you cool. Masks can also be a little harder yet to tolerate for heavily bearded men. (But don't shave it. Have some dignity.)

In regard to my clothing, there is always that one thing that seems to sneak up on me during turkey season... Oh, yeah! Spring. And yes, it gets hot out there, people. When making an educated guess in gear choices, find something that keeps your body cool!

One of the reasons I love spring gobbler season is because I don't freeze my ass off the whole time I'm out there. It's always nice to actually enjoy the good weather when out in the woods instead of making the hunt a constant battle of hot versus cold. Planning your layers of clothing and camo can be tough. Choosing underlayers, socks, shirts, and adding the final camouflage touch can be tricky to keep affordable, but overall, you need to be prepared for the season ahead. Spring can have some crazy mood swings, and your frosty morning can quickly become a hot sunny day in the blink of an eye. It's always easier to take layers off than put them on, so start thick. But actually be sure to take them off when the time comes. (It took a while, but after my first mild heat stroke from a long hike back, I realized that I don't want to experience it twice.) I have been backpacking during my hunts for the last few years in my old age. Doing this has allowed me to go much farther into the woods than I was as a young, inexperienced man, and I will say it has paid off more times than not to have somewhere to put all my extras!

All in all, I don't think hiding is as scientific as some people make it out to be, but being skilled at it is a true art. Use a little common sense and avoid the shiny, pick good and simple patterns, and do everything you can to prevent sweating. Getting uncomfortable due to poor planning will ruin more hunts, regardless of whether it is a turkey hunt or not, than almost anything else I can think of. I honestly think making the right camo choice is that easy. When hiding in the woods and trying to stay unnoticed by the wandering eye of some big tom, I would rather rely on instinct and being still than rely on how much money I spent on clothes to show my buddies up.

3.3 Gauge Your Confidence

I briefly touched on an important topic earlier in the book when I mentioned that hunters often set their own handicaps while pursuing their animal of choice. This is all part of a hunter's idea that there has to be a "fair chase" between them and the animal they are trying to harvest. Oftentimes, with deer or other big game, the caliber of the firearm is always in hot debate, especially when it comes to whitetail. In Pennsylvania, there are the .30 caliber guys who can't ever believe that their 30-06 is in any way, shape, or form replaceable.

We hear it all the time in the hunting community, "My daddy hun-ned wit a turdy a'ught six and so 'ave I and so 'as lil' Jim Bob, an' et neva a gone change."

Yup, and those guys knock them down year after year, and they do great. But my brother (a grown ass man) hunts with a little, short-barreled .243, and I'll be the first to admit that it does more damage than my (preferred) .308 has ever done to a deer. I have never seen his intended target walk away from him in all my life. Big thanks to my dad and other family and friends for teaching us to be good shots, but *for Pete's sake*, sometimes once the rifle becomes so "high powered," I'd be willing to bet that the debate has to stop somewhere. My experience is that a rifle's effectiveness becomes nothing more than what someone gets comfortable and confident with.

So, how does this play into turkey hunting?

Well, the shotgun has quite a few choices when it comes to deciding on how someone wants to pursue the wild turkey. I personally hunt with a trusty, pump-action, 12-gauge that shoots a full choke and can load 3.5-inch magnum rounds. This shell packs in a high number of BBs that scatter into a specific pattern while flying through the air toward their target. In the world of turkey hunting, there are no solid bullets like you would see from a traditional rifle. These guns are made to hit a large area over a large range. Sounds like a lot of information to the newbie who isn't familiar, but let me do my thing and provide some education.

First off, hunters have a few choices when it comes to how they want the firearm to function. Many hunters go for the pump-action gun first. A shooter's left hand is supporting the gun (obviously, this would be if they are right-handed), and each time they pull the trigger, a single shell goes off. The shooter then manually slides the mechanism back toward themself to discharge an old shell and "rack" a new one in the chamber. When the shooter slides the mechanism forward, that new shell is loaded into the chamber and sealed tight. Might be a lot to read on paper, but a shooter will pretty much move naturally into the following shot. I like this style of shotgun for the idea of safety; each time I shoot, I am in control of when the next shell goes into the gun. Then, I repeat if necessary. Although I wouldn't admit it to most of my hunting buddies, if I did.

This gun is totally different from a semi-automatic, which is also legal to hunt with, as long as it holds no more than three shells in the tube (in PA). With this style, each time you pull the trigger, a gas-powered mechanism slides back to do the ejecting and reloading for the shooter. One trigger pull gives you one shot. These are great for hunting, and even better for some of the trap and skeet-obsessed shooters out there trying to keep a smooth and consistent follow-up shot for the next clay pigeon or, sometimes, missed turkey.

Lastly, hunters could go for a break-barrel gun that holds just a single or double shell. These are by far the most iconic in nature, definitely something you might see in the movies, as they have a bit more character and style. When a sportsman wants to load one of these, the barrel is literally broken by pressing a lever at the back of the gun's chamber, and then the barrel drops off on a hinge. You slide the shells into place and then close it back up. Once that is done, you're ready to shoot. By limiting the amount of shooting opportunities, many hunters use this style of shotgun to really stretch the "one shot, one kill" mentality that many outdoorsmen strive so hard to achieve. If you know you don't have a follow-up shot, discipline becomes a huge factor when you're considering pulling the trigger.

Believe it or not, I don't know a single hunter who wants to find out they put a bad shot on any animal. I have seen whole hunts ruined for some people who believe they have caused that animal any sort of pain. (There is much more humanity in hunting and being connected to nature than the non-hunter may think!) So making a good choice with what gun they use is really important. I actually shot my first pheasant with a single-shot 20 gauge when I was a young man. This gun was a hand-me-down from my great-grandfather, manufactured in the 1920's. To this day, I don't know if my dad was trying to prove a point or just working with what he had when he forced me to use this gun, but you can damn well bet that I did *everything* I could to make that shot count when I got the opportunity! If you don't get to make a choice like I did here, be disciplined and practice!

The second main choice hunters make is probably the biggest limitation of them all. Hunters have to choose to work with a specific caliber, or in this case, gauge. The gauge of a shotgun is the bore diameter of the gun's barrel and directly correlates with how many BBs are packed into the shell. This choice is largely based on the hunter's comfort level with the amount of power that gauge may or may not have. I personally chose a 12 gauge. Why? Well, it's not too scientific for me. It's a good middle-ground firearm that is available in my area. If I need shells, parts, modifications, or other, there are abundant items for me to choose from. Plus, the gun just has enough *"umph"* that it seems to take down the animals I am interested in harvesting, from squirrels to turkeys. I have no concerns.

Honestly, until very recently in life, I have always been used to working with what I got, so I am happy to have been able to choose my shotgun. My friends often ask me why I hunt flintlock season with a .58 caliber roundball rifle, and my answer is simple: I got it from a guy for 125 bucks! The standard in black powder rifles is a .50 caliber, as supplies are widely available, and it's a large enough bore to take down medium to large game. My .58 becomes an oddity because only a few sizes exist over the .50, and manufacturing of the supplies is very limited. Many states actually have a size requirement for hunting, so if you are interested in this niche style of hunting, be sure to check out your state's regulations.

Anyhow, other gauges of shotgun do exist. Most of the time, youngsters start off with a .20 gauge. This caliber is smaller than the .16 or .12 and does a nice job for small game hunting, or even turkey hunting if you can get the bird close enough. Many parents choose it for its availability, as it's a common caliber, and because it won't rip their son or daughter's shoulder off in the first six shots of practice. Many adults choose this model because it's lightweight, and the smaller caliber adds a bit of skill into the mix. Anything light and easy to carry in the woods is always going to attract a crowd as far as guns and gadgets go.

Some of the crazies go smaller yet. There is a gauge that has been used forever but has recently gained a good bit of popularity, this being the .410. It racks a cartridge similar to a .45 caliber pistol bullet in diameter, but of course, in this case, the shell is longer. Some gun manufacturers have even fashioned the .410 shell into a pistol for self-defense. What someone thinks they may be defending themselves against with it is questionable, though! These guns have to be choked to extra, EXTRA full chokes, and they require a good bit of calling skill to get a bird in close. These guys and gals that take on the challenge of hunting birds this way are a special breed and have to devote a grand amount of time to practicing their shooting skills. Many are experienced hunters looking to make the game challenging and have a great story to tell over Thanksgiving dinner when the family gets together. Small shells mean they probably get to pick fewer BBs out of their teeth when eating, so I'm sure that makes grandma happier, too.

Just like a drummer choosing their cymbals or a runner having a preferred set of running shoes, a hunter has to choose a caliber or gauge that they are comfortable and skilled with. In each of these instances, prices, availability, and knowledge come into play, so there is no reason not to start off with a hand-me-down starter gun. My beforementioned deer rifle, the .308, was given to me in 8th grade, and honestly, at this point, I have no reason to replace it, even when the new fancy guns on the shelf are calling my name. Work with what you can reasonably get your hands on, and then get out and harvest an animal, turkey or not. Practice with it, and when you take the shot, be able to feel good about what happened that day. Our time spent out in the forest has to be well spent, and if a hunter comes back with a sick feeling in their stomach, that's no good for anyone. It's inevitable that something won't go your way at some point in your hunting career, but do everything possible to limit that. Make a choice, however it pans out, and like all things in life, run with it.

There are plenty of ways to take on a hunt when choosing your firearm, and not everyone agrees on the method of taking down an animal. I know tons of people who despise archery hunters because they see people who get lazy, or make bad shots at animals, and so on. I, for one, couldn't touch a target after I had suffered a back injury. So I took the time to research and invest in a crossbow. That choice has given me more joy, time in the woods, and confidence than anyone could ever imagine.

Don't agree with me? Stick to rifle season!

Do you think rifles take too many animals out of the breeding population? Try hunting with a muzzleloader or with buckshot in a shotgun!

Don't want to shoot female turkeys out of the breeding population? Stick to jakes and toms.

There are a lot of options out there, and I think the non-hunter would once again be surprised at the limits we outdoorsmen (and outdoorswomen) put on ourselves when it comes to taking an animal for harvest. These limits go far beyond the gauge of a shotgun. It comes back to the idea of our "fair chase" while pursuing game.

So, why are so many people worried about the choices that hunters make? Maybe it's because that choice is made by a neighbor, friend, or co-worker, and skeptics of hunting see the result of that choice. Yes, we kill animals, but I've said it before and I'll say it again: if someone can mindlessly buy meat from the grocery store and not think about it any more than that, why should they care? My deer, turkey, or bear that I harvested had a good life, felt nothing, and provided something important for my family in a way that I felt was done in a moral fashion. What's wrong with that?

I once again ask these people to talk to the hunters nearby and say, "Hey! What's the story about that one?" or, "How did you get that deer, or turkey, or bear?" I bet that person will light up when they tell all about the hunts, gear, and the story behind whatever firearm they inherited from their grandpappy, uncle, or wily ancestor (be prepared for a long story if that's the case). If someone asks me about the subject, most of the time I'll even try to pawn some homemade snacks off on them. Kind of a win for the parties involved, in my opinion, and I do really love watching others enjoy the meat as much as I do. Many times, our skeptics find that hunters are, in truth, honest and excitable people who like to share knowledge and stories of their hunts. All they have to do is ask.

Finding the right gauge for a shotgun is just a place to start when it comes to jumping into the subject of how someone *chooses* to hunt! Confidence is key when hunting for the elusive North American Wild Turkey, so hunters had better know what their follow-up will be when that big tom steps out.

3.4 People Are Strange

It's an honest-to-goodness truth that all of us are a little weird.

Really, we should all ask ourselves what is normal. Are the neighbors normal? Am I normal? Are your co-workers normal? (Not a chance.) Here I am, sitting around, furiously clicking away at the keys on my keyboard to air grievances about turkeys and acting as if I am some kind of scholarly researcher. All while hoping that I will get results in the field because of it.

I won't pretend that this is normal. I mean, why would it be? Webster's dictionary describes normal as "conforming to a standard, type, or regular pattern, or being characterized by what is considered typical, routine, or usual."[4] Honestly, that sounds a bit boring to me. We all have our quirks, and hunters are no different. In our regular lives or hunting routines, for that matter.

Think about a tennis match on television? The server seems to always have some kind of pattern they follow before hitting the ball.

Bounce it a few times, take a look, bounce again.

Breathe in, breathe out.

Toss the ball in the air.

And yell as loud as they can, in some act of intimidation toward the player on the opposing side, as they hit the ball across the court.

Play the point, rinse, and repeat until someone wins their set.

Just like them, hunters have some weird routines and ways to get the luck flowing before heading out into the wilderness, and I thought I would share some of mine: the good, the bad, and the ugly. Who knows, maybe the guys at hunting camp will seem a bit more normal after this?

My first (and probably most childish) of several hunting taboos is that I don't believe I can get out in the woods and see results unless I have a cookie breakfast. It feels good to get that one off my chest. Whoo! (Yes, hi. My name is Jake, and I am addicted to cookies—more specifically, chocolate chip cookies.) It's simple but very important that I do this. And if my wife makes her world-famous chocolate chip cookies, those are a big luck booster. Get a little love mixed in there before heading out into the woods, and it will be a good day. However, other chocolate chip cookies will also do the job. I have rankings for the brands, but let's not get into this right now. Suffice it to say that they probably aren't as effective as they should be. I'm willing to settle if I have to. I'll only dip these cookies in black coffee (my daily preferred drink), and after dipping enough cookies to make me happy, I'll suck down the rest of the cup of coffee and head out into the woods. No cookies most likely means that I won't get a deer or turkey that day. Regardless of whether this routine is effective or not, my sweet tooth definitely isn't letting go of this one.

Many hunters, gymnasts, and powerlifters, and then some, have a lucky meal, shirt, or charm. I have even seen people change clothes during a football game or switch what they are eating or where they are sitting to get the Pittsburgh Steelers going in the right direction.

"*Yinz* are doing great out there now that I am wearing green instead of red, go get 'em boys!" This is probably what a good bit of Steeler Nation is thinking at any given time. Makes sense, right? I've watched grown men go to bed during a football game, just because they thought it would help their team win. My cookies don't seem so odd after all, when you think about it.

On a more serious note, the second taboo I have about hunting has to do with bad luck. A little backstory here: when I was fourteen, my dad and I were hunting whitetail on some state game land near my grandfather's house. Coming up empty for the morning sit, we decided to go with a classic deer drive, where one person is the "walker" and the other is the "watcher." It was a simple plan. I would go into the valley and sit near an opening where we typically liked to watch for critters. Then, my dad would make a loop around me in a small radius across the top of the hill, hoping to push a deer down into the valley where I could see it. Hunters do something like this all the time with mixed results, but it's a proven tactic for larger game like whitetail or bears that gets the animals moving, for better or for worse.

So, I said, "Sounds good, dad. I'll make sure the radio is on in case you need me." Then came a period of waiting, and I felt like I was coming up empty again. I was underneath a big pine tree, looking out into a clearing near some beech brush and dressed like the great pumpkin. That had to guarantee a deer, right? Next thing I knew, the woods went from dead quiet to what felt like a marching band coming at me through the beech brush. Sticks breaking, trees shaking, water vibrating in my bottle just like the movies—the whole nine yards, really.

I prepared myself, tried to calm my breath, and—*oh shit!*—I saw the silhouette of a big black bear crashing through the beech brush, coming straight at me. She was a big mother, too. (Not like that.) I mean, Mama had three cubs in step behind her. I think I tried to shrink my body as much as I could at this point against the tree truck I was sitting against, hoping she wouldn't see me in my brightest safety orange. Everything I learned in hunter safety and past experiences in the woods told me that I was in trouble if those cubs got too close to me.

The big mama bear stopped about fifty yards in front of me and started to look like she was ready to defend her turf. I could see her eyes frantically scanning the landscape, and I could hear her sucking the air through her nose, hard, and breathing out the same way. She smelled someone, and she didn't want them there. The next thing I knew, she stood up on her hind legs, looked around one last time, and then hit the ground running, making a beeline straight at me.

Son-of-a-bitch, what do I do now?

I sat as tight as I could, but she was full bore at this point. When she got within twenty yards, I did what I had to do and cracked a shot with my .308 off the hip in hopes that the sound would scare her. A log right in front of her blew up, and in a sea of sawdust, she turned hard to the right, cutting away from me down through the valley. At the same instant, I jumped to my feet and ran as fast as I could toward the clearing on my left. I thought getting out in the open was my best chance to see what was happening and make an escape if I had to. As soon as I looked back, the three cubs were on my heels, and I figured I was a dead man (teenager).

I didn't think I reloaded, but to my surprise, I had another bullet in the chamber. In a rush, my shaky hands ejected a full round, and I didn't have time to get the next one in. I stopped running when I reached the clearing, slid the last bullet into the chamber, and turned back to the bears, not knowing if I was going to have to shoot the only round I had left.

I froze, locked in place. The bears were right on me. Each of the three cubs ran a full circle around me, curiously bumping into me at my legs as if to tell me I was in *their way*. I was in their woods, not the other way around. Then, in an instant, they turned back and disappeared with Mama into the big hemlock trees and far into the valley.

I tried to radio my dad multiple times afterwards, but the reception was bad, and all he was hearing was a bunch of beeps and static.

So naturally, when he got back to me and heard a shot, his first reaction was to ask me, "What the hell are you down here making so much noise for?"

Thanks, buddy.

I was pretty freaked out and could barely get my story straight. And by this point, I'm also not even interested in being quiet or trying to preserve what is left of our hunt.

I got my ass chewed out for a few minutes, and after I calmed myself enough to explain the story, we both got our heads on straight and took a look to make sure I didn't wound the big mama bear. Thankfully, she was safe, ready to raise the cubs into adulthood without a scratch on her. The weirdest part of the story, though, was that after all the hoopla, a doe quietly stepped out into the clearing when we sat to take a drink of water. My dad wasted no time and knocked her down, completing the hunt for the day. Time to get my ass in gear and start dragging this deer back to camp. What a morning.

So, why tell all of this? First, my family loves to hear my bear stories, as I have had far too many close encounters. I'm concerned that they are my spirit animal, and a close friend of mine actually believes that it could be a sign from above. I am a little afraid that she's actually right at this point, and her "test of bravery," as she describes it, is ongoing. Why didn't I get something cuter? Or more vegetarian? Second, you needed this whole backstory to make sense of my next point.

This bad-luck hunting taboo I have is that any night in hunting season from there on out, if I have a dream about black bears the night before, I don't hunt on the following morning. I take it as an omen from my subconscious that says to me, "It's not safe to swim today." And I am not willing to take the chance to prove, or disprove, that something could go wrong in the woods that morning. To hell with bravery. I'll happily find something else to do with my time and be constructive elsewhere. Those deer, turkey, grouse, or *whatever*, weren't expecting me anyway, and I figure they will still be there later on. This little quirk worked out one time when I shot my first buck with a crossbow. I had a dream of a black bear peering through a berry patch directly at me, so I slept in. That morning was rainy, and I was late going out after my wife talked me into getting a morning hunt in. Within fifteen minutes of hiking out into an old cut corn field, I killed a little seven-point. It was a long shot, but he went down in about twenty-five yards, and I couldn't have been happier. If I had gotten out there while it was still dark, who knows what kind of story I would be telling!

There is good luck, bad luck, and changing luck. The last major taboo I have is a way to change the tide of the hunt when days are slow, and there are too many hours left out in the field. To do this, I suggest pulling up a good chair inside the hunting blind or taking a quick walk back to camp. Coffee is the key for this one, so pony up and make a cup, because my final hunting taboo is to have a 'caffeine nap' to change my luck. (Remember the part where I said this whole chapter wasn't going to be normal?)

This whole thing is starting to sound like a sort of double negative. Well, what it is really is a race to beat the clock. I get myself nice and comfortable during a morning break and have a strong cup of, hopefully, percolated black coffee. Drip coffee will suffice, but it just doesn't have the same steamy allure about it. After downing the cup of joe, I attempt to fall asleep for a little bit and rest my eyelids before the caffeine kicks in. A perfect nap should only be about twenty to thirty minutes to hit the sweet spot. After I wake up, the caffeine kicks in, and I get my hunting gear back on. When I'm back at it out in the woods, I feel like a million bucks. It's really unbeatable.

I am in no way, shape, or form a nutritionist, nor am I giving any dietary advice (a lawyer will probably tell me to say this at some point, so I'm sticking it in here), but it's a perfect way to change my bad luck into something better. Caffeine naps will get any hunter "ready to rip," as my brother would say. My dad, brother, and I would routinely meet at our camper back in the day, after a morning sit in our treestands. My dad would fire up the percolator on top of the propane stove. Shortly after, we would have a cup of coffee or maybe a snack, and then we'd get our rest in before hitting it hard until dinner time. I'd like to say, more often than not, one of the three of us would pull through and put some meat on the table that night.

Strange? Weird? *Taboo*, even? Yeah, but then we all have something, of that I'm sure. However, if any of these work and someone sees results, then maybe the luck factor is real. Many hunters tell me that a large part of hunting is being in the right place at the right time. There is just good luck for hunters and bad luck for the target animal of choice. And that's okay. I'd like to think that a little luck, the right technology, and some know-how are what really go into making the pursuit of the animal worthwhile.

Although now that I think of it, maybe this doesn't apply to turkey hunting at all.

Or at least, so far it hasn't for me.

Part 4: In Conclusion and for Conservation

How does someone end a story that hasn't ended in real life? This is hands down the hardest chapter of the book for me to write thus far. We all have stories to tell and experiences to share, and let's face it, when people like me spend enough time out in the woods, you end up with some odd or unique experience that makes it all worthwhile. That's what brought me here in the first place.

Am I special?

Probably not.

Do I hope that what is special to me is conveyed through the pages of this book?

Yes, absolutely.

I don't care if my readers are anti-hunter, average Joes, or if they are hunger-driven meat-eating machines.

I think we can all agree that people have their passions, and it's good to share those passions with other people around us. I also think that calling attention to the non-stop survival machines known as the North American Wild Turkey can only be good for them. I'd like to believe that the idea I have of sharing my love for the turkey will only push others to hopefully care about them just a little bit more. After that, who knows? Awareness is a great first step to action, in my opinion.

So, how do we conserve the vital American resource we know as the wild turkey? Honestly, when it comes to the conservation of any game animal, I think it just starts with general knowledge of the critter. (Here comes my decade of being a teacher. I'm sorry.) Through my years of hunting, fishing, biking, hiking, and what have you, I have naturally become more knowledgeable about the subject by experiencing it firsthand. I also quickly develop preferences for the areas where I like to enjoy each of these sports, whether it's a scenic and calm stretch of river on the kayak or a hike that has a great view at the end. When we were in school as kids, we were taught to study. So why not study the hobbies we enjoy as adults? Where to go, how to do it, what other people like, and the list goes on if you want it to. If turkeys are the resource I am passionate about conserving, then hunting, reading, researching online, and talking to others who are versed on the subject is an obvious square one. Only then can I compile the right gear and resources to make my attempts successful in the field. The experience part of all this comes with time and relentless dedication.

People who are interested in hunting should also consider getting involved at a local level. Sportsman's clubs and other similar wildlife groups are a great place to start if you have no other place to go on your own. Or if that is too big of a jump, just ask a neighbor or close family member to show you the ropes. Other subjects unrelated to hunting apply here, too. Want to save a species of plant? Learn the basics first and know where and how it grows. Love dogs? Help out at a shelter and learn how to properly care for one. General knowledge of any subject and a good network of people who have that knowledge can be worth a goldmine.

On an individual level, the things closest to us are the ones we have the greatest ability to make an impact on. I am far more worried about my turkeys here in Pennsylvania than someone in Texas or Oklahoma should be. They should likewise be just as concerned about their group of thunder chickens. If ever I got rich and famous, I'd be far more willing to spread my wings and help them out, but the chances of that are probably slim to none. I do, on the other hand, have a chance to control use of family property, guide hunting trips with friends, and influence local legislation without much effort.

One of the simplest ways we can take control is by choosing to pay attention to what goes on around us in planned land development, agricultural activities, and silviculture (logging). Each of these important economic fields have their own set of regulations on both the state and federal levels. These regulations help identify best practices and safe resource management of an area. Anytime someone builds a structure, from a home to a new skyscraper, the earth loses some amount of landmass that wild critters call their own. Even though this construction is a necessary part of human progress and growth within our culture, we need to be mindful that our new housing development is well planned, maintained, and has the best interest of the earth in mind.

Effortless concepts that could go into farming and logging, like leaving mature trees with low branches or windbreaks along vulnerable areas, can provide important habitats for turkeys and other animals. When a housing development is under construction, are the workers controlling water runoff so animals have safe water sources downstream to drink from? It can be that easy to identify and let the right people know if it's not the case. Many companies now even have environmental teams that take the work extremely seriously because of this whole concept. If looking to hunt on local farmland, talk to the farmer and see what his or her long-term goals and interests are for their land. It's quite possible that they may be more open to the idea of letting some woods grow up or dedicating a small area as a food plot for the wild animals than some might think.

A simple sales pitch is all it might take for them to make a huge impact on their local wildlife population.

Land and animal conservation can come in many forms. These are simply things that I think about on a regular basis. As a former woodworking teacher, I love to see a nice straight tree get turned into a beautiful cabinet. As a turkey hunter, I love to see that big straight tree come out of a well-managed forest that keeps the next brood of turkeys healthy and happy. Each side of the coin is as important to me as the other, which makes it hard to explain to people new to the subject.

The last thing that I think is good for conservation efforts is not just for turkeys, but also for whatever wild animal a person has a passion for. It's as simple as being nice. "Nice guys finish last," has to be, in my opinion, one of the biggest bullshit lines I have ever heard in my entire life. When two or more people get into an argument with someone or enter a debate of some sort, the fastest way to lose is to lose your temper and get angry. So when someone asks questions about hunting, fishing, or responsible herd management of a species, we as hunters need to take it upon ourselves to not take it as an attack. When we are approached by a fish commissioner or game commissioner, there is a high likelihood that they aren't trying to "poke the bear," as some would say. Not all, but many of them are genuinely interested in how we are doing that day and hoping to see the best results from the time spent in the woods.

And if that's not the case and something is wrong, maybe it should be viewed as a teachable moment instead of an opportunity to play the victim.

Each of us, as hunters, fishermen, or outdoorsmen and women, should take time to teach, explain, and offer knowledge to those who don't have it or are seeking it. We should be offering to take our nieces and nephews hunting if their parents don't go, or offering advice on the shooting range to someone new to the sport. We never know when we might be handed the opportunity to make a difference in someone's life, but we definitely won't if we don't try. If you are just lucky enough, that person you helped will do the same for someone else someday.

So, as I conclude my ongoing story, one very stark similarity of my current turkey situation comes to mind. In the movie *Escanaba in da Moonlight* (a timeless classic), actor Jeff Daniels plays a character named Reuben, a hunter in the Upper Peninsula of Michigan who is introduced to us as "The Buckless Yooper." Sometimes I feel like Reuben. He's constantly surrounded by well-traveled hunters who seem to make bagging a buck year after year look easy. Then, to prove he's not jinxed, Reuben begins to work harder at the pursuit of the animal that is important to him and his family. Willing to do whatever it takes, at the end of the movie, all his craziness pays off, and he has his day. But I won't spoil the fun, as I highly recommend watching the movie.

With that said, until I have my day, let's just say it's been one hell of a journey. The turkeys are still out there, and so until that changes, I will be too. As I continue my relentless pursuit, I will always remain thankful for the countless people and memories that have come along with my hunt for the North American Wild Turkey.

[Note to future self... Insert first turkey hunting success story here]

4.1 I'm Not Done Yet

I wanted to leave you something for reference and your continued research on turkey hunting. Partly organized. (I'm trying to look like a professional here.) The real takeaway of all this is to give one last disclaimer, as we have come to the end: please don't just take my word for or believe anything previously read in this book. God knows I haven't done myself any good.

Notes from the reading:

[1] According to the American Museum of Fly Fishing, Thoreau is actually *misquoted* as saying this. Although it is attributed to him as one of his most famous quotes, it appears to be more of a summarization of ideas he has throughout his texts and journal entries. At the end of the day, I just like the "quote."

Brunvand, Jan Harold. "Famous Thoreau Quotation Is Pretty Fishy." *American Museum of Fly Fishing*. June 13, 2025. Accessed September 12, 2025. https://www.amff.org/famous-thoreau-quotation-pretty-fishy/

[2] Ben Franklin actually wrote the letter to his daughter, but didn't formally rally for the turkey to be the national bird over the bald eagle, as a later reference in my text suggests. This is according to The Franklin Institute, but I doubt any of their researchers were alive back then to really know the truth.

The Franklin Institute. "Did Benjamin Franklin Want the National Bird To Be a Turkey?" *The Franklin Institute*, May 21, 2024. https://fi.edu/en/science-and-education/benjamin-franklin/national-bird

[3] This Act is officially called the Wildlife Restoration Act of 1937, according to the U.S Fish and Wildlife Service. Not only does it collect tax revenue for maintaining habitats, but it also funds hunter education.

U.S. Fish and Wildlife Service. "Wildlife Restoration." Last modified September 16, 2025.

https://www.fws.gov/program/wildlife-restoration

[4] Being normal isn't any fun, but unfortunately, here is a very normal dictionary link.

Merriam-Webster. "Normal." *Merriam-Webster.com Dictionary*. Accessed September 23, 2025. https://www.merriam-webster.com/dictionary/normal

In order of appearance:

<u>Henry David Thoreau</u>
Poet and philosopher. See his works, such as "Walden," at any local library.

<u>Benjamin Franklin</u>
Author, writer, politician, and founding father. Hopefully, you paid attention in history class.

<u>Colonel Tom Kelly</u>
Author of *Tenth Legion* and many others. Visit his website at: tomkellyinc.com.

<u>Steven Rinella</u>
Outdoorsman, founder of MeatEater, Inc. Author of: *Meat Eater: Adventures From The Life of an American Hunter*, *American Buffalo: In Search of a Lost Icon*, and more. Connect with his content at: themeateater.com.

<u>Jim Shockey</u>
Videographer and outdoor writer. See him on the

show *Jim Shockey's UNCHARTED* on the Outdoor Channel.

Jeff Daniels
Comedian, author, and director. Watch *Escanaba in da Moonlight* on an available streaming service.

Turkey species, facts, and hunting information that aided in the writing of this book:

"B&C Member Spotlight - C. Hart Merriam." *Boone and Crockett Club*. 2024. https://www.boone-crockett.org/bc-member-spotlight-c-hart-merriam

Kaufman, Kenn. "Wild Turkey." *Audubon*. 2025. https://www.audubon.org/field-guide/bird/wild-turkey

Kennamer, Mary C. "Gould's Wild Turkey." *NWTF Wildlife Bulletin*, no. 5. National Wild Turkey Federation, September 9, 2009.

Martin, Scott. "Wild Turkey Overview." *All About Birds, Cornell Lab of Ornithology*. Cornell University. April 5, 2025. https://www.allaboutbirds.org/guide/Wild_Turkey/overview

"Merriam's Turkey." *Oklahoma Department of Wildlife Conservation*. 2024. https://www.wildlifedepartment.com/wildlife/field-guide/birds/merriams-turkey

Neary, Ben. "NMDGF Biologists to Talk About the Gould's Turkey Ahead of Once-in-a-Lifetime Hunt Deadline." *New Mexico Wildlife Federation*. January 7, 2023. https://www.nmwildlife.org/news/nmdgf-biologist-to-talk-about-the-goulds-turkey-ahead-of-once-in-a-lifetime-hunt-deadline?rq=Gould

NWTF. "Subspecies of Wild Turkey." *Mossy Oak*. March 6, 2025. https://www.mossyoak.com/our-obsession/blogs/turkey/subspecies-of-wild-turkey

"Osceola Wild Turkey (Meleagris gallopavo osceola) – A Wild Turkey Profile." *Project Upland Magazine*. May 12, 2023.
https://projectupland.com/turkey-hunting/osceola-wild-turkey-meleagris-gallopavo-osceola

"Rio Grande Wild Turkey." *Texas A&M AgriLife Extension*. 2024. https://wildlife.tamu.edu/wildlifemanagement/turkeys

"Turkey." *Commonwealth of Pennsylvania.* 2024. https://www.pa.gov/agencies/pgc/wildlife/discover-pa-wildlife/turkey.html

"Wild Turkey Fact Sheet." *PBS.* July 26, 2021. https://www.pbs.org/wnet/nature/blog/wild-turkey-fact-sheet

"Wild Turkey (Meleagris gallopavo)." Species & Habitats. *Washington Department of Fish & Wildlife.* September 20, 2025. https://wdfw.wa.gov/species-habitats/species/meleagris-gallopavo#desc-range

About the Author

Jacob Pistner is a lifelong resident of Pennsylvania and currently lives in Elk County, with his wife, Hope. He graduated from California University of Pennsylvania with a degree in Technology Education K-12, and he worked for a decade as a teacher in the public school system. During his time as a teacher, he coached cross country and track and field. Jacob is an active outdoorsman who loves hunting and fishing and enjoys woodworking, reading and spending time with family.

For more information, you can contact Jacob at nawt_book@yahoo.com

www.ingramcontent.com/pod-product-compliance
Lightning Source LLC
LaVergne TN
LVHW041844070526
838199LV00045BA/1433